THE
HANNAH
ANOINTING

MICHELLE MCCLAIN-WALTERS

CHARISMA
HOUSE

Most CHARISMA HOUSE BOOK GROUP products are available at special quantity discounts for bulk purchase for sales promotions, premiums, fund-raising, and educational needs. For details, write Charisma House Book Group, 600 Rinehart Road, Lake Mary, Florida 32746, or telephone (407) 333-0600.

THE HANNAH ANOINTING by Michelle McClain-Walters
Published by Charisma House
Charisma Media/Charisma House Book Group
600 Rinehart Road
Lake Mary, Florida 32746
www.charismahouse.com

Unless otherwise noted, all Scripture quotations are taken from the New King James Version®. Copyright © 1982 by Thomas Nelson. Used by permission. All rights reserved.

Scripture quotations marked AMP are taken from the Amplified Bible. Copyright © 2015 by The Lockman Foundation, La Habra, CA 90631. All rights reserved. Used by permission. Text in braces {} in the AMP was added by the author.

Scripture quotations marked AMPC are from the Amplified Bible, Classic Edition. Copyright © 1954, 1958, 1962, 1964, 1965, 1987 by The Lockman Foundation. Used by permission.

Scripture quotations marked ESV are from the Holy Bible, English Standard Version. Copyright © 2001 by Crossway Bibles, a division of Good News Publishers. Used by permission.

Scripture quotations marked GNT are from the Good News Translation in Today's English Version—Second Edition. Copyright © 1992 by American Bible Society. Used by permission.

Scripture quotations marked KJV are from the King James Version of the Bible.

Visit the author's website at www.michellemcclainwalters.com, michellemcclainbooks.com.

Library of Congress Cataloging-in-Publication Data:
An application to register this book for cataloging has been submitted to the Library of Congress.
International Standard Book Number: 978-1-62999-567-0
E-book ISBN: 978-1-62999-568-7

This publication is translated in Spanish under the title *La unción de Ana*, copyright © 2019 by Michelle McClain-Walters, published by Casa Creación, a Charisma Media company. All rights reserved.

19 20 21 22 23— 987654321
Printed in the United States of America

CONTENTS

Introduction

YOU ARE THE ANSWER

> For the creation waits in eager expectation for the children of
> God to be revealed.... The whole creation has been groaning
> as in the pains of childbirth right up to the present time.
> —Romans 8:19, 22, NIV

THE EARTH IS groaning. Can you hear it? Issue upon issue. Crisis upon crisis. Disunity, dishonor, and disrespect. Addiction, murder, and suicide. Depression, anger, and bitterness. Fear, worry, and discontent. Epidemics of the heart, mind, soul, and body threaten the fabric of God's creation.

Who has the answers? Where are the children of God who will lead the next movement to find them? Who will lead the next move of God? Who will lead the next move to end inequality among races and genders? Who will step forward and end poverty, homelessness, and hunger? Who will speak peace and prosperity among the nations? Who will deliver the word of the Lord and bring healing? Who will mend broken hearts? Who will love the unlovable? Who will liberate the oppressed? Who will bring joy where there is heaviness?

The earth is groaning. Can you hear it?

The Lord has been speaking to me about a company of women arising with answers in their belly. The books I have been writing for the last several years highlighting outstanding women in the Bible have been an outpouring of the revelations God has been giving me about the unique and unsubstitutable impact of women who know their purpose and destiny, know how to discern the times and seasons, and are activated, unified, and supported in their missions.

I am confident of this: God made no mistake in creating women with the ability to give birth to the answers our world is hungering and thirsting for. He made it so not only would we give birth, but we would also do it in due season, in the fullness of time. God is an on-time God, and He delivers on His promises at the right time—not too early and not too late. His promises to deliver, heal, increase, and bring peace and salvation are fulfilled through us in two ways:

1. The natural/physical/generational birth—You could be raising the next generation of world changers. Your natural children and your children's children could be the answers.

2. The birth of your dream/purpose/destiny—The thing that God has put on your heart to do could be the thing that changes the world: books, businesses, ideas, cures, and other innovations.

There Are No Limits on Your Fruitfulness

Some of us are so used to being limited by man that I bet you looked at those two items and began to think of which way God wants to deliver His promised seed through you. Well, I am here to tell you that you don't have to choose which way you will be fruitful. Both are part of the essence of who you are, and women are created to do both with style and grace. The tricky part comes in managing them effectively by discerning and responding to God's plan within God's perfect time and being confident in who you are.

If you are insecure and lack confidence in the areas where you are called to reproduce, people inside and outside the kingdom of God will cause you to think that you have to choose one or the other, that you cannot have all that God has promised. People are quick to offer their opinions and impose their convictions on what they think your call should look like. It is important for Hannahs to remain focused and confident in God and His promises to them so they are not distracted by the multitude of voices that could lead to doubt. They must be willing to think outside the box of culture and know that in God there are no limits. We are anointed to be fruitful and to multiply in all areas of life.

Look at the women who went before you. Some of them gave birth to natural children, spiritual children, and culture-shifting movements simultaneously. Some did one or another. Some you know well; others are everyday women whose names are not mentioned in history. Look at Noah's mother. We don't know her name, but we know she gave birth to and raised the only man alive who feared God at that time and was counted as righteous. (See Genesis 6.) By faith he built the ark and saved the human race from being annihilated by the wrath and judgment of God (Heb. 11:7). Abraham's mother, who is also unnamed, gave birth to the father of many nations. God blessed Abraham and promised to bless us and all the nations of the earth through his seed. (See Genesis 17; 22:18.)

Rebecca gave birth to Jacob, whose name was changed to Israel after he wrestled with God and prevailed. His twelve sons were the leaders of the tribes of Israel. Rachel gave birth to Joseph the dreamer, who was sold into Egyptian slavery and went from a prison to a palace, all to prepare the way for the people of God to be saved and protected from famine. Jochebed gave birth to Moses, the one who delivered God's people out of Egypt and led them to the land God promised them. King David's mother, though unnamed, raised the greatest king who ever lived, a friend of God and one who established an eternal movement of praise and worship. Mary gave birth to Jesus Christ, the Savior of the world.

Then there's Miriam, Moses' sister, who gave birth to extravagant prophetic worship, with instruments, song, dance, and utterance—even before King David was born. (See Exodus 15:20.) Esther gave birth to a bondage-breaking prayer movement. Deborah gave birth to spiritual children—prophets, judges, and war heroes.

And then there is Hannah. She gave birth to Samuel, who was one of the greatest prophets and whose words never fell to the ground (1 Sam. 3:19). He restored prophetic order among the people of God and ministered to kings.

Generation after generation, women have been giving birth to people and movements that shake the world. This continues today with women who give birth to and nurture our culture shifters; science and technology giants; Nobel Peace Prize winners; world-changing leaders; songwriters, authors, and artists who create things that move us; and pastors, evangelists, and revivalists who preach, teach, and heal with the fire of the Holy Ghost. Women do this on the front lines and behind the scenes.

It's the enemy's strategy to put limits on women and the value we bring to spaces we occupy. He's skewed the playing field, made the opposition seem greater than it is, and played us against our flesh. But there is a high calling that dwells within women alone. Men were not created to do what women do. But it is not only our biological predisposition to give birth to natural children that enables us to initiate new life. Our biology points to a deep spiritual significance women hold in the earth, the kingdom, and eternity.

From babies to businesses, we are carriers of new and glorious things God desires to release in the earth. We carry within us the promise of the next president, pastor, or CEO, or of a God-given solution to the problems, issues, and tragedies we see in our world every day. There is a deficit in the land, and modern-day Hannahs are the carriers and deliverers of the promise that will fill the gaps and release the power and glory of God in our lives and communities.

What Is the Hannah Anointing?

One aspect of the Hannah anointing is the ability to harness the essence of what it means to be a woman and break through the enemy's attempts to shut up the womb. In the beginning God created woman to be home to generations of people who would fill the earth with the holiness, beauty, and glory of God. With man, woman was charged to be fruitful, to multiply, and to subdue the earth (Gen. 1:28).

Another aspect of the Hannah anointing is the spirit of endurance. The Bible says the one who endures to the end will be saved (Matt. 24:13) and will receive what is promised (Heb. 10:36). The word *endurance* in Greek is *hupomone*. It means "constancy, perseverance, continuance, bearing up, steadfastness, holding out, patient endurance. The word combines *hupo*, 'under,' and *mone*, 'to remain.' It describes the capacity to continue to bear up under difficult circumstances, not with a passive complacency, but with a hopeful fortitude that actively resists weariness and defeat."[1]

Modern-day Hannahs will stand on the promises of God and will not be swayed by the criticism of others. They will be relentless in the face of doubt. They will not settle for anything less than the will of God for their lives. The Hannah anointing is the ability to tolerate and hold up under pressure and persecution, never yielding the posture of faith in the promises of God. It is

the ability to never lose courage under the pressures of unful-
filled promises.

Hannahs know who they are. They are confident. They are
God-assured rather than self-assured. They are persevering, persistent, resilient, humble, prayerful, prophetic, and nurturing.

The name Hannah means "grace" or "mercy,"[2] though it didn't
seem as if either one was active in Hannah's life since we find
her suffering through a season of barrenness. Hannah, which is
the Hebrew word *Channah*, also means "entreaty" or "prayer."[3]
Channah is connected to the word *channowth*, which means "to
intreat, to pity, be gracious."[4] Both Hannah's name and *channowth* come from the Hebrew root word *chanan*. This word
means "to be gracious, show favour, pity," or "properly, to bend or
stoop in kindness to an inferior; to favor . . . causatively to implore
(i.e. move to favor by petition):—beseech . . . (be) merciful . . . have
pity upon, pray, make supplication."[5]

Not only does Hannah's name signify who she was, but it is
also descriptive of the position she took before the Lord while
petitioning for His promises to manifest in her life. She bent, or
stooped, low in the presence of God in prayer, crying out to Him
to give her a son. She sought after and beseeched His favor and
implored Him to show her mercy.

Hannah prayed, she persistently and relentlessly pursued the
promise of God in her life, and she would not let go until the
Lord blessed her. She stood in the face of torment, mocking, and
being misunderstood for the way she prayed. She withstood the
temptation to compromise, settle for what she had, and give up
on her dream of having a son. Hannah's story is the prophetic
archetype for women everywhere to pray and never lose heart
until they see a release of the promises of God, until they see the
enemy's hand lifted off of them, and until they see the spirit of
barrenness broken and fruitfulness returned.

Through Hannah's story you will see how it is not only the biological birth of a seed that brings the answers you seek. The answers to our persistent prayers of faith and petition are coming in both natural and spiritual forms. There are many women who were once barren who will birth children, but there is still more to Hannah's story that we can learn from. If you have labored long in prayer over a dream, a business, or a breakthrough idea, could this too be your Samuel? Could the fulfillment of your dream and primary purpose be what changes everything?

Modern-day Hannahs carry within them the answers people are crying out for. In Hannah's time the people of Israel were in a spiritual drought and had not heard from God for a long time. Hannah was desperate to bring forth a son. Little did she know that while she was praying for her own desires to be fulfilled, God was preparing her to birth the man who would start a prophetic movement that would change the world and who would be the connecting force that would bring God's people back into fellowship with Him.

Woman of God, the answer to your prayers is coming. Do not relent. Resist discouragement and distraction, and be resilient in the face of setbacks and failure. Do not be afraid to try and try again. The season of barrenness you are experiencing is not what it may appear to be on the surface. God will answer and give you the desires of your heart. You will see the fruit of your labor.

Hindrances to the Hannah anointing

As we study Hannah's story through a prophetic perspective, it will become clear that these six characteristics formulate spiritual artillery that comes against the Hannah anointing:

1. Jealousy as personified by Peninnah's unnerving taunting and torment

2. Rejection that comes as a result of extended periods of unanswered prayer

3. Compromise proposed through the words of Hannah's husband, Elkanah

4. Judgment and criticism as seen in Eli's response to Hannah's praying in the temple

5. Shame from society's judgment in Hannah's day against women who could not bear children

6. Temptation toward pride and retaliation after the promise has manifested

How Hannahs Get Victory and Become Fruitful Again

Hannah made a vow to God that unlocked an overflow of multiplication and increase. She shifted her focus from self and used her anguish to persevere until her barrenness was broken. Hannah was a prophetic picture of what happens when a woman pours out her heart to God. Modern-day Hannahs will release a cry of desperation that releases the realm of miracles. This grace will require the following:

Endurance

As I mentioned earlier, Hannahs are known for their ability to endure and stay focused on the promise of God for their lives. This is a key to breaking through seasons when the Lord shuts down production in our lives. It is the main key for overcoming jealousy, temptations to compromise and settle on something less than God's ideal, and ungodly judgment and criticism aimed at your situation.

Prayer

Hannah persisted in prayer, returning to the temple year after year. She found strength and validation in the house of the Lord. She persisted in maintaining three important postures for breakthrough: resistance, relentlessness, and resilience.

Agreement and partnership

The grace of Hannah turned a potentially upsetting interaction with the priest Eli into one of agreement and blessing.

A new vow

Hannah's time in prayer led her from a place of wanting a child for her own fulfillment to wanting a child for service to the Lord. God honored Hannah's vow as she tapped into the power of surrender. In response to her surrender God released to her an overflow of multiplication and increase.

Chosen by God

Hannah was chosen by God to display grace and humility in action. What do you do when you're chosen by God? What do you do when the dream of your heart is also the dream of God's heart? The joy and the pain of being chosen by God are mind-blowing and terrifying at the same time—you are chosen by God for a great task, but you are completely in the dark while you are being prepared. This is where trusting in the Lord is challenged. My life's confession is this: When I don't understand the workings of God's hand in my life, I will trust His heart of love toward me.

God has called and chosen us to advance the kingdom in partnership with Him, but we could never imagine in our wildest dreams where submitting to His will can lead us. The process one has to go through as a chosen one requires faith, patience, endurance, humility, and pure trust in the ways and doings of the Lord. His ways are not our ways.

To walk in the Hannah anointing, it's going to take a turning of the cheek in the midst of persecution. Standing in faith, believing the Word of God against all odds and every natural circumstance and even what sometimes looks like defeat, is not an easy task.

Hannah was a woman chosen by God to birth Samuel the prophet. Her barren condition paralleled the barren condition of Israel. There wasn't a prophetic voice in the earth. The Scriptures say, "The word of the Lord was rare in those days; there was no widespread revelation" (1 Sam. 3:1). Hannah did not know that her intense burden and intercession for a son was moving in tandem with the heart of God for a prophetic voice to be released in the earth.

I believe the dream God placed in your heart is the dream of His heart. There are many problems that need solutions, and God will use modern-day Hannahs to birth them. He will use women who have gone through fiery trials and testing to bring great deliverance to their generation. They will see miracles and provision. They will know fruitfulness and fulfillment that can only come by the hand of the Lord. Modern-day Hannahs will experience enlargement and authority in the natural realm as well as the spiritual realm. They are the ones who will hear "Daughter, the God of Israel has granted your petition as you have asked of Him." (See 1 Samuel 1:17.)

Hannah had an overcomer's heart of faith. Her heart of faith carried her through difficult situations in life that would have destroyed others. The trying of her faith produced patience and endurance. She developed the victory that overcame the world through her faith. This is the heart of Hannah, and I challenge you to tap into it. When you do, you will see cycles of barrenness,

lack, and fruitlessness, whether physical or spiritual, break off of
your life. It is God's desire to see you walk in the fulfillment of
your heart's deepest desire. What are you praying for that has yet
to manifest in your life? To what lengths are you willing to go to
see the promise of God fulfilled in your life?

God is raising up women with a Hannah anointing who have
the desperation to cry out until fruitfulness returns to their lives,
the tenacity to fight against the disappointment that comes in
times of waiting, and the courage to surrender the very thing
they have prayed for. These are the women who will see the birth
of the promise of God manifested in their lives and in generations to come.

As we take this journey together through the pain and shame
of barrenness and infertility, both in the natural and in the spirit,
I declare to you today that your season of barrenness is tempo-
rary and coming to an end. You will not suffer long. You will not
be put to shame. The Lord your God will fight for you. You need
only to stand still and see His salvation. Your promised seed is
on the way.

Prayer to Activate the Hannah Anointing

*Father, thank You for empowering me with the spirit
of endurance. I decree that I am strengthened with all
power, according to Your glorious might, for all endurance and patience. I take authority over all the spirits of
mind control and mind-blinding spirits. I release Your
power over my life and my situation. Let this be a day
of breakthrough. Let this be a day of Your glory.*

*I command every spirit of limitation, spirit of bar-
renness and lack, and spirit of python to be bound now
and to loose my mind, will, and emotions in the name*

of Jesus. I stand against any attempts to sabotage and squeeze the life out of the promise of God over my life.

Father, I pray for Your glory and Your grace to be released to me. Heal me and return my hope in the future and the destiny You have outlined for my life. Bring me to a place of breakthrough, for You are the breaker. You have gone before me. I bless You and put You first. I remember Your name, O God. Your name is great and greatly to be praised.

I decree that every muzzle that's been on my praise is broken today. I decree that the high praises of God will be in my mouth and the two-edged sword in my hand. I take authority over the spirit of slumber and apathy. God, I pray that You would send Your consuming fire into my life and ignite my heart to praise You and to prophesy of Your power, protection, and deliverance, just as Hannah did. Let there be fire in My praise where the devil has tried to take the hallelujah out of my mouth. I will bless the Lord at all times. I shout hallelujah!

Chapter 1

CLOSED FOR A SEASON

Now there was a certain man of Ramathaimzophim, of mount Ephraim, and his name was Elkanah....And he had two wives; the name of the one was Hannah....He loved Hannah: but the LORD had shut up her womb.

—1 Samuel 1:1–2, 5, KJV

MANY WOMEN—MARRIED AND single—deal with the pain and shame of not being able to have their own children. Married women endure cold, invasive doctor visits; suck in their breath as they are stuck for the millionth time with painful hormone shots; and shed tears over the negative result of yet another pregnancy test. Single women who've lost count of the years they've been waiting on the right mate also want to feel the joy of motherhood. They go to God not only for a mate but also to join in the cry for sons and daughters. In both cases the disappointment and shame can be suffocating.

That God would deliberately shut down fruitfulness for a time in a woman's life is hard to imagine, but that is exactly what He did with Hannah and with some of us today. Sometimes God has to shut down production for a season to do the proper maintenance, upgrades, renovations, and other kinds of spiritual, emotional, mental, or physical repairs needed for us to be in optimal condition to receive and steward the next level of increase and multiplication He is about to pour out.

Maybe you've seen the following signs on some of your favorite shops or restaurants: Closed for Repair, Closed for Maintenance, Closed for Remodeling, Closed for Renovation, or Closed for Inventory. This is disappointing when you were craving your favorite dessert or there was an outfit you saw in the window last week that you came back to get. But you know if you are patient, your favorite place will come back better than before— with a better menu, updated decor, or special deals and discounts to more than make up for your short-term loss.

There are seasons in our lives when God has to shut things down in order to prepare us for the next big thing about to be released in our lives. Our current capacity can't handle what God is about to do, so He closes up shop for a season to prepare us for expansion and increase.

We need to shift our perspective on the issues of shutting down the womb, delaying the birth of new things, and halting reproduction, fruitfulness, and multiplication for a season. Though it can feel shameful or as if God has forgotten about you, the first thing you need to do is understand that God has your best interest at heart.

"'For I know the plans and thoughts that I have for you,' says the LORD, 'plans for peace and well-being and not for disaster, to give you a future and a hope'" (Jer. 29:11, AMP). He desires that in every way, we succeed, prosper, and be in good health (3 John 2). He takes great pleasure in the prosperity of His servants (Ps. 35:27). He loves to hear and answer your prayers (Prov. 15:8). He loves to come to your rescue (Ps. 34:19). So anytime He calls for a shutdown, He is doing it with great love and care for you and intention toward the plans He has in mind for your future.

Though God will share His secrets with us concerning our lives, He doesn't always tell us everything all at once. We don't always see the full picture of what God sees. But we can trust Him in the unknown because of what we do know of His love and faithfulness. We can be confident He is always orchestrating our lives so that all things will work together for our good (Rom. 8:28). I love how the Amplified Bible says it:

> And we know [with great confidence] that God [who is deeply concerned about us] causes all things to work together [as a plan] for good for those who love God, to those who are called according to His plan and purpose.

There are other parts to this as well that we are going to look at concerning seasons of barrenness and coming into the due season for fruitfulness. We are also going to explore when God calls for a shutdown in production so that you can experience the blessing of divine rest and deep worship.

Aligning With God's Timing

We cannot always assume that just because we have been prophesied to, it's our season and we are ready for what's coming. We must instead realize that God is strategic—there is a due season and a fullness of time around which He orders the events of our lives if we are surrendered to Him. This is good news and a comfort to the woman of God who trusts God and knows the times and seasons of the Lord. This means your season of barrenness is in God's hands and He is orchestrating the outcome. Your barrenness is not in the hands of the enemy, with you about to lose grip as random and traumatic attacks are launched at you. No! God is working in the details of every twist and turn so that both you and your seed come to an expected end.

God had a place and time for Samuel to be born just as He has a place and time to fulfill the promise He has seeded in you. He shut Hannah's womb so He could work in her heart and prepare her to be the mother of one of the greatest prophets ever to live. If it had been easy for Hannah to bear children, she may not have found herself in the sanctuary of the Lord year after year, seeking His face and crying out to Him. It was in those times that God was able to develop her character and share with her His plan for her promised son. Imagine if Samuel had been born while Hannah was still in the mind-set of having a son for her own joy and pleasure. We would not have had the Samuel we honor to this very day—the one who reconnected the people to their God after a long spiritual drought, the one who established a prophetic order that led God's people for centuries.

This is why it is so important for Hannahs to embrace God's timing even in a season when it seems as if He is not answering. Faith and trust lead you to say, "Though I don't always feel as if this is true, I know my God hears every one of my prayers and collects every tear I shed. He hears me, and He is answering. I stand on His promises."

I know this is a hard season, beloved, but I challenge you to press in to God. Ask Him to help you understand His timing for your life. In my book *Prophetic Advantage*, I talk about the difference between our natural chronological time—*chronos* in the Greek—and *kairos*. I'll come back to this in the next chapter with a fresh perspective and how it relates to Hannah. And then in *The Deborah Anointing*, I use seasons—winter, spring, summer, and fall—to bring light to the spiritual seasons we go through in our walk with God. I believe Hannah was in the midst of her winter season. See if this reads like what you are going through:

> Your spiritual winter can seem like a time of darkness, as if your life is unfruitful, and you may assume your dreams are dying. But during winter there is no fruit bearing. It is a time when God kills everything in your life that will affect the harvest of the next season in your life. Spiritual winter is the most uncomfortable time for

many Christians. However, this is a season to redefine and further develop a relationship with the God of your call. This is when God continues to develop your root system in Him. There He will give you directions for planting new crops in spring, which is the next season. Spiritual winter is the time for evaluation, planning, and preparation. It is a time for letting go of anything that will destroy your call [or your seed]. It is also the time to learn the uniqueness of your call.[1]

Though there is pain in this season, there is also much comfort to be found in that God is working in you to will and to do according to His good pleasure, plans, and purposes (Phil. 2:13).

What's Wrong With Me?

Even as your spirit discerns the divine purpose in seasons marked by lack, nonproductiveness, and unfruitfulness, your soul—your mind, will, and emotions—may need more time to catch up and submit. In Genesis 1:28 God gives the creation mandate to Adam and Eve: "Be fruitful and multiply; fill the earth and subdue it." When one is not able to fulfill what should be a natural order of God, the first question that arises in the heart is, What is wrong with me?

Hannah and her family were deeply devotional in a time when the nation was in deep depravity. As they journeyed to the temple of the Lord year after year to offer burnt sacrifices and worship, society had become a cesspool of corruption with murder, gang rape, compromise, and idolatrous living at its peak. Hannah's neighbors were wicked and somehow still prospering and fruitful, while Hannah and her husband were living in social disgrace and not seeing the fulfillment of God's promises even though they were careful to follow all the religious protocols of the day.

Barrenness was the ultimate tragedy for a married Hebrew

woman. It left her feeling humiliated and ashamed. Family members, neighbors, and friends always had something to say about the childless woman, calling attention to her lack of favor with God. Shame is a painful feeling, and it is mainly about how we appear to others (and to ourselves). It doesn't necessarily depend on our having done anything to deserve it. Still, the spirit of shame makes you feel flawed and unworthy. This opens the door to feeling rejected by God and questioning His love. Yet, beloved, these are times when you must put your trust in the Lord and remember what the Word says:

> Instead of your shame there shall be a double portion; instead of dishonor they shall rejoice in their lot; therefore in their land they shall possess a double portion; they shall have everlasting joy.
>
> —ISAIAH 61:7, ESV

When Barrenness Is Ordered by the Lord

Yes, the Lord had shut Hannah's womb! On the surface that just doesn't seem right, but if we are going to understand the truth behind Hannah's life story, we need to get revelation on what it means when God orders a shutdown. A shutdown can bring peace when we clearly understand that the closing of Hannah's womb was not the work of the devil. God was in control of Hannah's destiny. The hand of God was orchestrating the events of her life. The fact that God had shut her womb reveals that God was in control, and if He shut her womb, He could also open it.

We must understand that God is also orchestrating our lives. Our dreams and motives will all be tried by fire. There is something that God is birthing in the lives of women—our understanding of His commitment to expand our capacity to carry the promise and see fruition. To effectively navigate these times of uncertainty, women will need to be completely sold out to the plans and purposes of the Lord.

Modern-day Hannahs will live lives of total obedience to the Lord. They will answer affirmatively the Lord's question "When I come, will I find faith in the earth?" (See Luke 18:8.) Hannahs are women who have walked the path of faith and total dedication to the will of the Lord. They are women who know they have been chosen by God, which means they know they have given up their right to privacy. Their lives are on display to show God's glory.

Shut it down and worship.

Many times I am baffled at the ways of God. There was a time in my ministry when I had a preach-to-live mentality. I would take inventory: "OK, I have four meetings, and I'll be given this amount of money. I have this much to pay..." I know ministers aren't often this transparent, but I am keeping it real so you can know that I am not writing this to you from some distant place; I lived this.

We know how we are. We tally and multiply, subtract and strategize, sometimes far in advance of what God has perfectly and divinely planned. When I was in this mode, I remember the Lord saying to me, "Uh-uh, I want you to shut it down. All I want you to do for the next six weeks is worship Me. Shut it down."

"But God, I have so much already in the works."

"No. Shut it down."

The first few times God spoke to me this way, I went back and forth with Him about my own plans, though I ultimately submitted to His command. Now when I sense His call to be still, I immediately respond by saying, "Yes, Lord, I'm doing too much. I have gotten ahead of myself," and I shut down whatever I have going on and worship.

Beloved, that is the hardest thing to do. To be the Mary in a Martha world is so challenging for us in this day and age. (See Luke 10:38–42.) To choose the better thing and sit at the feet of Jesus instead of being busy doing what seems like the most naturally strategic thing at the moment is not easy.

This is another aspect of a God-ordained season of barrenness when God calls you away to still your striving and rest in Him while He recalibrates your vision. The Lord had to get my attention because although I had been fruitful and received His promise of a ministry, I did not have the right mind-set toward it. He called me out for it, and I am grateful because while my spirit said, "Yes, God, it is all Yours," my flesh was fighting for control and to make it work the way I saw fit.

Listen, there is a way that seems right to us (Prov. 14:12). We are a people full of resources, ways, means, and intelligence. The hardest thing to do is put down what feels natural to us when our backs are against the wall. The usual response or action, the usual weapon, and the usual strategy will not work when God says, "Shut it down."

Stand still and rest.

If you've been faithfully serving the Lord for many years, then you know how easy it is to go right to your spiritual defaults. When trouble comes, you know how to war in the spirit. You know how to call your prayer partners. You know how to get to that conference or revival and get under some corporate glory. You know how to decree and declare. You know how to take up the shield of faith and the breastplate of righteousness. But do you know how to stand still? Do you know how to rest? Rest is a weapon too. This is not about being lazy but about finding a place of rest in the Lord. If you can get this revelation, then you'll see that rest is another aspect of your winter season, when the Lord is saying, "Sit this one out. You don't need to fight this battle. Take your position, but stand still, worship Me, and witness My salvation."

Chosen to Bear Fruit

These are the days when God is awakening many women to their destinies. This is a season when we are going to get a revelation about the scripture that says, "Many are called, but few are chosen" (Matt. 22:14). God calls us to walk in destiny, but we have to decide to live a life of discipline and worship, a life that is pleasing to the Lord, in order to go to that chosen status.

These are the days when God is aligning your life. As you come into the presence of God, as you pray and cry out to Him, saying, "I want to move into my calling. I want to live according to my destiny. I want to bear children. I want to be the mother of a movement," I believe the Lord hears you and is working within you the will to bring it to full term. He is the One who put the longing in your heart to walk wholly in your call. His Spirit is the One stirring you to cry out, and He is the One who will bring breakthrough. He will cause you to suddenly experience seasons of fruitfulness even though you have been barren for so long. It is His desire for you to move past your own wants into hungering and thirsting for what He has for you. When you get in this position, your promise will spring forth.

John 15:16 says, "You have not chosen Me, but I have chosen you and I have appointed and placed and purposefully planted you, so that you would go and bear fruit and keep on bearing, and that your fruit will remain and be lasting, so that whatever you ask of the Father in My name [as My representative] He may give to you" (AMP). We often look at the success of others and wonder why we don't have success the way they do. Understand this: we did not choose God; God chose us first. I also want you to understand that you have been appointed. To be appointed means to be set, to be assigned. You have an appointment, an assignment from God, and a set time to see your purpose fulfilled and promise manifested.

God has appointments for success for your life. Don't let the enemy make you think God doesn't have success for you, that He doesn't have specific things for you. God says, "You have been chosen. I am the One who got this party started. I am the One who created you. I am the One who chose you to serve Me." Hannah knew this truth and walked confidently in it even in the face of Peninnah's fruitfulness, even though it seemed as if Peninnah was anything but concerned about the will of God for her life.

Can you stand on this truth while everyone around you succeeds and you are still waiting to see your promise manifest? Can you stay in the secret place of prayer and supplication, keeping your request before the Lord and gaining strength as you inquire at His temple, while still having genuine joy when others succeed?

God calls us. Many are called, but few are chosen. Why? Because of the way we respond. Many stay at the "called" phase, but you and I can move toward that chosen phase like Hannah when we respond to God with a full and sincere "Yes, God. Not my will, but yours be done."

When you do this, God takes you from called to chosen. He says, "You have been chosen to bear fruit." God wants to break the spirit of barrenness in your life. He wants to break the cycles in which you keep working and toiling but the ground will not yield fruit. The divine breaker has come to break every demonic curse of barrenness where you are not able to reproduce, do not have enough finances, or cannot do the things you want. By the power of God, you will bear fruit.

Then I love this: not only does He want you to bear fruit, but He wants your fruit to remain. Have you ever had really high highs where you see fruitfulness in your life? Things are flowing, your business is growing, you're doing well on your job, money is flowing, and your giving is flowing. But then you get fired, and you don't have a job, and the next years of life are in utter turmoil, and there's no more fruit. I decree that curses of barrenness and lack will be broken in the name of Jesus. Declare over yourself that you are chosen to be fruitful.

Hannahs Will Fulfill the Genesis 1:28 Mandate

We are supposed to be fruitful and multiply. That is part of the creation mandate (Gen. 1:28). As a woman who has been created by God, fruitfulness is in your DNA. It is part of His original plan. I decree that you are fruitful and will multiply and replenish the earth.

If you don't have enough revelation and you are not producing or reproducing, you cannot multiply, and you certainly cannot have dominion. The devil would love to keep you trapped in a place of shame, self-pity, rejection, and self-hatred. But this needs to break in order for you to operate fully as one who was created in the image and likeness of God. So in the name of Jesus, I call you forth to take authority over every demonic assignment of shame, self-pity, rejection, and self-hatred. There is no room for them in your life.

As Hannahs we can come against these seasons of lack, barrenness, and drought. We can break the drought. We can call down the rain. We can decree that all the hard, dry, and stony ground will be broken up. We can break the curse of the desert. We can prophesy to ourselves that we will be fruitful. We will multiply.

When God gives us things, we don't want to cast them away. When the harvest comes, we need to be sure to store up only what we truly need for ourselves and give away what's left to the world. We're supposed to be fruitful and multiply and fill the earth with God's power and glory.

This is the hour to fill the earth and subdue it. In order to subdue something, you have to be great in number. I believe that is why the devil works so hard, especially with Christians, to get us into a place of abortion. Some of you have been fruitful, but then the enemy came and tried to make you abort your destiny. I decree that the spirit of abortion is broken and you will bear fruit. You will fill the earth and subdue it. You will have dominion.

May this word be quickened in your life. May it not fall to the ground. May it not delay any longer.

Prayers That Loose the Spirit of Shame

Father, I thank You that I am fearfully and wonderfully made in Your image. When You made me, You made something beautiful. I loose myself from every spirit of shame. I decree that instead of barrenness, You are giving me fruitfulness. Your Word says, "When pride comes, then comes shame" (Prov. 11:2). Therefore, I humble myself before You.

Jesus, You bore shame upon the cross so I wouldn't have to. I rebuke the spirit of unworthiness and self-hatred. I will not be made a spectacle. I will not walk in shame.

Lord, I thank You that You are my helper. You rescue me from the spirit of shame. I keep my focus toward the throne of glory. Those who wait upon the Lord will never be put to shame. I cry out to You, O Lord, don't let me be put to shame. Don't let my enemies triumph over me (Ps. 25:2).

Prayers to Activate the Genesis 1:28 Mandate

Father, I thank You that Your word never returns to You void! Your word shall accomplish everything You sent it to do. I decree that I am blessed. My womb is blessed. My life is blessed. I break every demonic assignment of barrenness. I decree that I am fruitful in every good work. I am not cursed but blessed.

The anointing for multiplication is upon my life. I will multiply in every area. I will fill the earth with my ideas and concepts. My dreams will be realized. I believe for the unusual. I believe You for the unheard-of and outlandish blessing upon my life. I declare restoration in my life. I declare that everything that comes from my womb will subdue the earth. I declare that I will walk in dominion all the days of my life. I have authority in the name of Jesus.

Prayers That Open the Womb and Restore Fruitfulness

He gives the childless woman a family, making her a happy mother. Praise the Lord!

—Psalm 113:9, nlt

Creator of heaven and earth, I worship You! I am Your servant. Let me find favor in Your sight. You are the God who gives the childless woman a family. I ask in the name of Jesus that You open my womb. I believe that nothing is impossible for You! Let Your hand touch my womb and release life. I open my mouth and give You praise. For Your Word says, "Sing, O barren" (Isa. 54:1), and I know You take the foolish things to confound the wise. I humble myself under Your mighty hand, and You will lift me up in due season. Let Your resurrection power touch my womb. For by my own strength I cannot prevail, but by Your power I will overcome barrenness. I decree that the law of the spirit of life in Christ Jesus makes me free from the law of sin and death. Holy Spirit, quicken my mortal body with life. Empower my reproductive organs with life.

Lord, let the spirit of restoration be evident in my life. Restore fruitfulness to my life. The thief has been caught, and he must pay seven times. Hannah declared in 1 Samuel 2:5 that "even the barren has borne seven." Restore me seven times more. Make me, like Sarah, the mother of nations, and let my descendants rule the earth. I make a vow to You that I will give back to You for Your full use everything that is birthed from my natural or spiritual womb.

Chapter 2

UNANSWERED PRAYER— WELCOME THE WAIT

I waited patiently for the LORD; and He inclined to me, and heard my cry. He also brought me up out of a horrible pit, out of the miry clay, and set my feet upon a rock, and established my steps. He has put a new song in my mouth—praise to our God; many will see it and fear, and will trust in the LORD.

—Psalm 40:1–3

IT IS HARD to make it through certain seasons in life when no one, not even God, is offering any answers. In life's craziest moments we find comfort in knowing who, what, when, where, how, and why, even if our situation is not totally relieved. We *need* answers for everything, but that is not always how things work. God, as the all-knowing One, is not obligated to share with us every detail of what He is doing. Though He delights in sharing His secrets with us and is ready to respond when we call, He has good reason for releasing the answers we need when we need them, not necessarily when we want them. Understand that He is the Creator and we are the ones He created. In due season He releases exactly what we need to walk abundantly in all He has promised.

Isaiah 55:8–11 always gives me comfort when I am desperate to hear from God on a matter but it seems as if He is not speaking:

"For My thoughts are not your thoughts, nor are your
ways My ways," says the LORD. "For as the heavens are
higher than the earth, so are My ways higher than your
ways, and My thoughts than your thoughts. For as the
rain comes down, and the snow from heaven, and do
not return there, but water the earth, and make it bring
forth and bud, that it may give seed to the sower and
bread to the eater, so shall My word be that goes forth
from My mouth; it shall not return to Me void, but it
shall accomplish what I please, and it shall prosper in
the thing for which I sent it."

—ISAIAH 55:8–11

Whether or not we know the details of what God is doing in
our lives, we can trust that He sends a prosperous word out into
our future and that it will not return void. What He has promised you will come to pass.

Another thing that this passage hints at is the idea of seasons—seedtime and harvest, spring rain and winter snow. There
is a time when seed must be sown, the ground tilled and culti-
vated, and the weeds pulled. Then there is a time to gather it all
and eat the fruit. There is also rain in the spring season and snow
in the winter season. I discussed seasons and timing in the pre-
vious chapter, and I discuss it in almost all my teachings because
understanding the timing of the Lord increases our trust in Him
and His ability to deliver on His word every time.

Hannahs represent God breaking through the winter season
and delivering us into spring, when things that seemed dormant
come alive and flourish. The Isaiah 55 passage reminds us that
even the ice and snow from the winter have value in that they
melt, and from the water new life is birthed.

Do not underestimate the value of this season you are in. I
know how hard it is to pray while feeling unheard, unanswered,

rejected, and passed over, but allow the Lord to minister to your heart and heal the broken places so you can come into full alignment with His plan for you and your seed. In the midst of your pain, there is an answer. God hears you and will respond.

In the meantime we must learn the art of holy wrestling with the Lord. Jacob became a master at it. (See Genesis 32:22–32.) He hung in the fight the whole time and prevailed. He must have felt all kinds of emotions as he pushed and pulled against the strength of the unidentified man. Can you imagine what he may have been thinking? "Why is this man fighting me?" "What did I do to deserve this struggle?" "I can't win. He is too strong for me." "Will God come and rescue me?" But when the man could not prevail against Jacob, He used His supernatural power to injure Jacob, causing a limp Jacob had for the rest of his life. This act revealed the nature of the man, and Jacob knew that he had wrestled with God Himself. Then, in the midst of being stricken, Jacob cried out for a blessing.

Could this be you? In the midst of your pain can you look past the unanswered questions and the rejection and reach out to God Himself, asking Him to lay His hands upon your life and bless you the way *He* desires? All the pain caused by Jacob's struggle went to the background once he knew whose presence He was in.

Beloved, God is faithful. He is not like man; He cannot lie (Num. 23:19). So if God is faithful and true, why hasn't the promise been fulfilled? Let's take a scriptural journey over the next couple of chapters and look at some of the reasons that it seems as if the answers to your prayers have not been released.

Times and Seasons

It is He who changes the times and the seasons; He removes kings and establishes kings. He gives wisdom

to the wise and [greater] knowledge to those who have
understanding!

—DANIEL 2:21, AMP

God gives wisdom and knowledge about the changing times
and seasons of our lives. You can be assured that you have everything you need to make the transition to the next level. God is
moving us forward in our destinies. He is advancing us forward
into His purposes and equipping us for greater accomplishment
than we have ever known. Our question to Him should be, How
do I make the shift? One of the best ways to get ready for the
next thing God has for you is to be in tune with His timing and
understand where you are in that continuum. To start, you need
to know that there are three different kinds of time.

1. *Chronos* time

Chronos is a Greek word for *time* that refers to a general
season of time. It's the passage of chronological time that occurs
as we live our everyday lives, which can sometimes be uneventful,
routine, and mundane. During this time God allows things to
happen that develop faith and teach us how to wait on Him. In
chronos we learn how to contend for the promises of God.

In her chronos Hannah routinely went to the temple to worship day in and day out. She did everything that was required
of her. She served the Lord and honored her husband. For extra
measure, she endured the ridicule of Peninnah and responded
with silent grace.

God develops the endurance of modern-day Hannahs in the
season of general time. I know you may be thinking, "What
does that mean? I thought I was in the time of God!" Timing
has many elements to it. As we've discovered through Hannah's
story, God uses the passage of time to mature us so we can better
understand His purposes, which ultimately trump our initial

wants. We come to understand why He gave us certain desires and how He wants us to wisely use them upon their fulfillment.

In chronos God is working behind the scenes of our lives, preparing us for the greatest breakthrough we've ever experienced. This is when God teaches us how to be faithful in the little things so that He can make us rulers over much.

2. *Kairos* time

Within chronos time there are life-altering moments that catapult you into the center of your destiny. This is *kairos* time. Kairos is a strategic time. The Greek word refers to "a measure of time, a larger or smaller portion of time," meaning it can be "a fixed and definite time, the time when things are brought to crisis, the decisive epoch waited for; opportune or seasonable time; the right time; a limited period of time; to what time brings, the state of the times, the things and events of time."[1]

We need to understand that we do not live our everyday lives in kairos. It is a seasonal, strategic time that puts us where we need to be in God. Then we live at a new level of chronos until God allows kairos to occur again. Kairos is jarring and intense. There is a heightened sense of urgency within kairos. These moments are likened to the suddenlies of God. They force you to leap, to respond quickly, and though in some cases you've waited and prayed for them, they do not wait for you to get comfortable with the sudden change or opportunities they present. Though it is the right time, the season is open for a limited period. You must be ready to respond.

Kairos is a window of opportunity in which we are to respond to the thing God is bringing into our lives. Sometimes kairos can appear as breakthrough, where the floodgates of blessings burst forth—blessings such as financial increase, job promotions, miraculous healings, an open door that was previously closed, approval for land or property when denial was expected, or a positive pregnancy test after years of being told bearing children was not possible.

Kairos could also come in the form of a crisis. Some of the hardest moments in life cause a shift in our thinking, leading us down a whole new path of wisdom, knowledge, and understanding. Those moments cause us to take a close look at ourselves and where we are in our journeys with God. Spiritual deliverance— being set free from demonic oppression or possession—can be a kairos moment. Salvation can be a kairos moment—when all of a sudden you hit rock bottom, but instead of dying or giving up, you choose a new life in Christ. Some kairos moments bring us to our knees, seeking the face of God for help and revelation. Other kairos moments bring us to repentance. Kairos moments bring us to the right place at the right time to receive from God the right thing He has always wanted us to have.

Kairos is an epoch when things going forward look nothing like what has been left behind. An epoch is "an event or a time marked by an event that begins a new period or development."[2] God is bringing us to a place where new things, new opportunities, new birth, and new developments will come to pass for us. He is bringing us to a place where the former things—dryness, lack, rejection, compromise, or unfruitfulness—will pass away.

When Hannah went to the temple with her family, she responded to a kairos moment that put her in the right place for something to shift. Peninnah's taunts had become more than she could stand. She couldn't take the humiliation and embarrassment any longer. So she pushed aside her meal, went to the temple, and cried out to the Lord until she had no more words. She could have sat there and stuffed food in her mouth or run crying to her room or told Peninnah to shut up. But instead Hannah responded in the right way to the right moment in time that positioned her for breakthrough. She was sensitive to the timing of the Lord. While she prayed, sacrificed, and worshipped for years throughout her chronos time, the Lord readied her heart to respond to His kairos time. And at the height of her crisis—that opportune time—Eli noticed her and said the words she'd been longing to hear:

> "Go in peace; and may the God of Israel grant your petition that you have asked of Him." Hannah said, "Let your maidservant find grace and favor in your sight." So the woman went on her way and ate, and her face was no longer sad.
>
> —1 Samuel 1:17–18, amp

Hannah knew, in that moment, that the Lord had answered her prayers. The Bible says that after the family returned home, Elkanah knew his wife, Hannah; the Lord remembered her prayers; and Hannah conceived a son. Hannah named her son Samuel "because {she had} asked for him from the Lord" (1 Sam. 1:20, amp). Your kairos time is coming. Be ready to respond to it at a moment's notice.

3. *Hora* time

Hora is a Greek word that refers to "a certain definite time or season fixed by natural law and returning with the revolving year, of the seasons of the year, spring, summer, autumn, winter; the daytime (bounded by the rising and setting of the sun), a day; a twelfth part of the day-time, an hour, (the twelve hours of the day are reckoned from the rising to the setting of the sun); any definite time, point of time, moment."[3] This is different from *kairos* in that it is not a window of opportunity open for a limited time. *Hora* is about seasons, which are more fixed and definite, meaning they occur in predictable patterns. Then there is a word that is derived from hora, one that for me creates a full prophetic picture of hora time: *horaios*. This word is simply and literally translated as "blooming, beautiful." It also means "belonging to the right hour or season (timely), i.e. (by implication) flourishing."[4] The word *horaios* brings my mind to a verse in Ecclesiastes, and though it is in the Old Testament and would have been originally written in Hebrew, it helps me see how hora time is about the season in which God makes all things beautiful: "He has made everything beautiful in its time" (Eccles. 3:11).

When circumstances have come together—all the right events, timing, or people—the window of opportunity is finally seized, and you are living in a season of breakthrough, you are in hora time, and it creates a beautiful thing.

Let's look at another biblical example that helps describe this time further:

> Now Peter and John went up together to the temple at the hour of prayer, the ninth hour. And a certain man lame from his mother's womb was carried, whom they laid daily at the gate of the temple which is called Beautiful, to ask alms from those who entered the temple; who, seeing Peter and John about to go into the temple, asked for alms. And fixing his eyes on him, with John, Peter said, "Look at us." So he gave them his attention, expecting to receive something from them. Then Peter said, "Silver and gold I do not have, but what I do have I give you: In the name of Jesus Christ of Nazareth, rise up and walk." And he took him by the right hand and lifted him up, and immediately his feet and ankle bones received strength. So he, leaping up, stood and walked and entered the temple with them—walking, leaping, and praising God.
>
> —ACTS 3:1–8

The name of the gate is called Beautiful and is the Greek word *horaios*. Is it not fascinating that God in His sovereignty made sure that this gate was named using the word *horaios*, which not only means "beautiful" but is also connected to the right time?

When God is ready to make everything beautiful in your life and you are in the right timing of God, it is your miraculous time to be made whole. The man at the Beautiful Gate, the centurion's servant in Matthew 8:13, and Hannah—as well as many others who experienced miraculous healings, breakthroughs, and deliverances—came into their hora time. I believe that Hannah came upon her hora season when Eli agreed with her and her womb was at that same hour made whole. The spirit of barrenness was broken, she stepped through the portal of opportunity (kairos), and she accessed a point when the fullness of time could be manifested.

This, of course, is what we can look forward to, but what about right now, when you are still waiting for that kairos portal to open? What is happening with the prayers you are praying but not seeming to get an answer to? Let's look at that.

Patiently, Yet Actively, Wait

There are times when prayers are seemingly delayed, and I want to reiterate that it is during these times that God is downloading revelation about Himself that you will need on your journey to fulfilling your destiny. There is value in keeping the right perspective that you are waiting *with* God and not *on* Him.

Sometimes we take a passive approach during seasons like this, but the process of waiting is not passive at all. Waiting is an active process. You should still be serving the Lord. The Bible tells us that "those who wait on the LORD shall renew their strength; they shall mount up with wings like eagles, they shall run and not be weary, they shall walk and not faint" (Isa. 40:31). The word for *wait* used in this verse is *qavah*, and it is "the

word most often translated 'wait' in the sense of waiting on the
Lord....*Qavah* means (1) 'to bind together' (perhaps by twisting
strands as in making a rope), (2) 'look patiently,' (3) 'tarry or wait,'
and (4) 'hope, expect, look eagerly.'"[5]

In the active process of waiting, your heart, mind, and very
being are connecting to the Lord—reading and studying His
Word, praying without ceasing, worshipping, serving, giving,
obeying, submitting, and remaining open to His voice for any
instructions He may give. I believe in the times of waiting, your
vision is being purged of compromise, vain ambition, and impure
motives just as it was for Hannah. It is OK to wait on the Lord
to perfect you. In fact, it is imperative. Let God remove anything from your life that hinders your dream. Let Him test your
motives and see if there is any wicked way in you (Ps. 139:24). Let
Him humble and break you under the mighty power of His hand.
Let Him do this while your dreams are still small. Let Him do
this with you in private so you will not fall when you are on a
larger platform and more people and things are assigned to you.
Let Him do this now so you will be strong enough to sustain the
great things He is bringing you into.

We also have an opportunity to build hope and faith during
the waiting time. Waiting on the Lord builds hope in the Word.
Psalm 130:5–6 says, "I wait for the LORD, my soul waits, and in
His word I do hope. My soul waits for the Lord more than those
who watch for the morning—yes, more than those who watch for
the morning."

There are times when we are disappointed by life. People will
disappoint us, and husbands may not understand, but we must
learn to stand on the Word of God and put our hope in Him.
Hope is an expectation to see the goodness of God in our lives.
Waiting teaches us to have a firm foundation on the Word of
God. It doesn't matter how long and dark the night season may

be—when we have confidence in the Word of the Lord, we can stand confidently, knowing joy is coming in the morning and light is breaking through.

There is a peace that can develop through the waiting season as well. Waiting develops patience, and if you allow it, it can quiet your fretting. The enemy of waiting is fretting. When it feels as if evildoers—the Peninnahs—are having babies, birthing businesses and nonprofits, and getting ahead in many other ways while you are still waiting for the one thing you've asked of the Lord, fretting can feel like the right response. The enemy wants you to fret. But Jesus arises in the midst of your worry and says, "Peace! Be still!" When Hannahs wait, they are not afraid because they serve the One to whom the wind and waves submit. When Hannahs wait, they are strengthened. When Hannahs wait, they stay active by worshipping and ministering to the God they love and who loves them. Hannahs allow the time when it seems as if no answers are coming to be a time of purification of motives and a time of pruning, shaping, and aligning. When you tap into the Hannah anointing, you will welcome the wait.

Prayers for Peace While Waiting

Lord, I make a decision to rest in You. I will not allow stress and anxiety to overtake me. I rest in Your goodness and Your plan for my life. I will wait patiently for You. I will not fret because of the wicked who prosper. I will not retaliate or be angry. I am confident that if I ask anything according to Your will, You hear me, and if You hear me, I have whatever I ask for.

I decree the God of peace has crushed Satan under my feet. Let every negative voice be silenced in the name of Jesus. I loose myself from rage and fear of the future. Let the peace of God rule my heart. I will not compare

my process with anyone's. I bind the spirit of competi-
tion. I speak peace to my mind. I bind the spirit of the
wandering mind. I loose myself from wrath and anger
with God. I labor to enter into Your rest.

Prayers About the Sovereignty of God

Yours, O LORD, is the greatness, the power, the
glory, the victory, and the majesty. Everything in the
heavens and on earth is yours, O LORD, and this is
your kingdom. We adore you as the one who is over all
things. Wealth and honor come from you alone, for you
rule over everything. Power and might are in your hand,
and at your discretion people are made great and given
strength.

—1 CHRONICLES 29:11–12, NLT

Father, I am so grateful my times are in Your sovereign
hands. I lean into the counsel of Your will. I stand in awe
of Your ways. I trust You with my life. I declare that every-
thing is Yours. You are the Alpha and Omega in my life.
I don't have to be afraid of my future because all victory
and power are in Your hands, and You are watching care-
fully over my life. Everything in the heavens and on earth
is Yours, including my body, my vision, and my dreams. I
offer them to You as a living sacrifice. Strengthen me to
stand still and see Your salvation in my life. Lord, at Your
discretion people are made great. I thank You that You
are making me great and giving me strength!

Remember the former things, those of long ago; I am
God, and there is no other; I am God, and there is none
like me. I make known the end from the beginning,

from ancient times, what is still to come. I say, "My purpose will stand, and I will do all that I please."

—Isaiah 46:9–10, niv

I decree that the purpose of God will stand in my life. I decree that the plan and strategy of the Lord is being revealed to me. Lord, thank You for making Your plan for my peace, my family, and my ministry known. There is no one like You. You are the giver and sustainer of life. You never change. Your love cannot be manipulated by my success or failure. I am fully convinced that nothing can separate me from Your love. Nothing can keep me from realizing the promise in my life. What You have spoken over my life in eternity past stands forever. Your plans for me are good, and no one can reverse them. I will not remember former pain, failures, or defeat, but I will remember and meditate on Your delivering power. I thank You that You do as You please. I thank You that it is Your pleasure to prosper me. You are the God who gives me the victory!

Prayers of Submission to Timing and the Preparation Process

Lord, I thank You that You make everything beautiful in its time. There is a right time and a fullness of time for me. I break and bind the spirit of delay off my life. I decree that as I am waiting on the promise to be fulfilled, I will not waste time. I decree I value time. I will walk circumspectly and redeem time in my life. I seize every opportunity to learn from You, Lord. I will not waste time on self-pity, jealousy, or being envious of others. I will not waste time arguing with and questioning You. I humble myself under Your mighty hand, and You will exalt me in due season. You are a God who moves in cycles, patterns, and seasons. I thank You for the grace to yield to Your process.

I loose myself from control spirits. I submit to Your way. Lord, I ask that You search my heart and remove any selfishness. Remove any selfish ambition. I pick up my cross and follow You. My flesh dies daily so I may minister in the power of the spirit. I repent of pride. I resist the devil, and he must flee.

Prayers About Ministering to the Lord While Waiting

Lord, I find joy in fellowshipping with You. "O God, You are my God; early will I seek You" (Ps. 63:1). I love Your presence. My soul thirsts for You. My soul silently waits for You. You are my Rock and my salvation. Heavenly Father, I come to look for You in the sanctuary of my heart. Help me see Your plans as I wait on You. I want to see Your power and glory. I want to experience Your loving-kindness, for Your loving-kindness is better than life. My lips will praise Your name. I lift up my hands to You in total surrender. My soul follows close behind You. I abide under the shadow of Your wings. Your right hand upholds me. You are righteous and true. You are awesome in Your doings toward the sons of men. Blessed be God, who has not turned away my prayers or His mercy from me.

Chapter 3

DON'T GROW WEARY

And let us not be weary in well doing: for in due season we shall reap, if we faint not.

—Galatians 6:9, KJV

MODERN-DAY HANNAHS REALLY don't need to go far to learn how to react and respond while we wait for our desires to be given to us. Hannah gave us a road map to follow that will lead us right into our kairos and hora times. Hannah's view of God and how she positioned herself during her season of asking, seeking, and knocking are the most important pieces to her arriving at a place of supernatural breakthrough.

What You Need to Know About God

Hannah used her waiting season to further develop her relationship with the Lord. Because of the time she spent praying and seeking Him, Hannah solidified her understanding of the character of God. The evidence of this is in Hannah's prayer in 1 Samuel 2. Early in the prayer Hannah declared three things about God: God is holy, there is no one like God, and God is our Rock. We need to cultivate our understanding of these concepts during our waiting period because that will cause us to push through to victory. A proper understanding of these three things will help you gain the right perspective and bring you to a place of peace and trust while you wait for your Samuel.

1. God is holy.

Hannah declared that God is holy: "No one is holy like the LORD" (1 Sam. 2:2). *Holy* means to be set apart and marked as totally different. Women who walk with an anointing like Hannah will have holy assignments. God dwells in eternal holiness. His character is perfect, and He administers justice for all who trust in Him. This was an important perspective for Hannah to hold while waiting for something for such a long time. That God is just means He fairly delivers the right judgments to all, especially the ones He calls His own. Hannah knew what was rightly hers, and she held on to the unfailing holiness of God during the waiting process. God's holiness also means that He is not crafty—He doesn't lie, trick, or deceive His sons and daughters. He is righteous (Ps. 11:7), and there is not any shadow of turning in Him (Jas. 1:17). He can be trusted. He is dependable. Wholeness is found in Him.

2. There is no one like God.

God is sovereign. God is always in control. To be healed from barrenness required the miraculous power of God. There will be things built and birthed in the earth by modern-day Hannahs that will be hard but not impossible. With God all things are possible to them that believe. There is no other God that is solid, immovable, and dependable as Jehovah! In a society of pagan worship the nature of God was displayed in Hannah's life. His faithfulness to keep His promise to her has echoed through time.

3. God is our Rock.

Hannah declared that there isn't "any rock like our God" (1 Sam. 2:2). Hannah could have never proclaimed God was her Rock and Deliverer if she never needed Him to be just that. Rock represents stability and strength. Rock provides a solid foundation. The nature of God is revealed in His names, and multiple scriptures declare Him to be the Rock (e.g., Deut. 32:4; 2 Sam. 22:47; Ps. 18:46; 28:1; 95:1). God was the Rock of Hannah's life—her support, her foundation, and the cornerstone of her life. There was nothing else for Hannah to lean and depend on to see the fulfillment of her heart's desire. She had no answers—only a promise to stand on—after years of praying for the same thing. The people in her life weren't really there for her. Peninnah was insensitive and mocking. Elkanah didn't quite understand her tears. And Eli thought she was drunk. She had to stand on the Rock.

God was the foundation upon which she built her faith, shaped her prayers, and managed her expectations. And in the process she learned more about who God is.

Know God for Yourself

When you have walked with the Lord for any length of time, you may feel as if you know Him. But I have come to understand that God will give us fresh revelation about Himself in the midst of waiting for the promise to be fulfilled.

Ephesians 1:17–19 (AMP) states:

> [I always pray] that the God of our Lord Jesus Christ, the Father of glory, may grant you a spirit of wisdom and of revelation [that gives you a deep and personal and intimate insight] into the true knowledge of Him [for we know the Father through the Son]. And [I pray] that the eyes of your heart [the very center and core of your being] may be enlightened [flooded with light by the Holy Spirit], so that you will know and cherish the hope [the divine guarantee, the confident expectation] to which He has called you, the riches of His glorious inheritance in the saints (God's people), and [so that you will begin to know] what the immeasurable

and unlimited and surpassing greatness of His [active, spiritual] power is in us who believe. These are in accordance with the working of His mighty strength.

God wants you to be confident in who He is. He wants you to know the immeasurable depths and unlimited greatness of His love. Hannah saw Him as holy, her Deliverer, her Rock. Who is God to you during this season? Yes, you have a promise, you have a prophetic word, but you have to get behind the what and into the who.

Dry, barren seasons are great teachers. These times help us loose any idolatry surrounding what we are praying for. These seasons allow us to get back to pure worship of our Deliverer. Though there is not one good thing He withholds from those who love Him, God is also teaching us to seek His face before we seek His hand. He calls us to know His character before we see His promises delivered. Again, this is about building the faith and endurance we need to get us through the many seasons of life with God.

It is upon this revelation of His character that God will show Himself strong on your behalf. This must be a personal thing. When Jesus asked His disciples who people were saying the Son of Man was, they called out a few names that sort of represented the anointing on Christ's life, but it was third-party knowledge—things they had heard. So Jesus asked, "Who do you say that I am?" (Matt. 16:15). Maybe the disciples were confused, or perhaps searching looks passed between them. Maybe there was some discussion back and forth about what Christ meant. But when Peter opened his mouth and declared, "You are the Christ, the Son of the living God" (Matt. 16:16), Jesus said:

> Blessed [happy, spiritually secure, favored by God] are you, Simon son of Jonah, because flesh and blood (mortal man) did not reveal this to you, but My Father who is in heaven. And I say to you that you are Peter,

and on this rock I will build My church; and the gates
of Hades (death) will not overpower it [by preventing
the resurrection of the Christ]. I will give you the keys
(authority) of the kingdom of heaven; and whatever you
bind [forbid, declare to be improper and unlawful] on
earth will have [already] been bound in heaven, and
whatever you loose [permit, declare lawful] on earth
will have [already] been loosed in heaven.

—MATTHEW 16:17–19, AMP

Do you see the power that was released to Peter because of
His personal revelation of who Jesus was in His life? He received
the full authority of the kingdom of God—to bind and loose the
things of the kingdom into the earth realm.

Like Hannah, are you waiting on the promise of a baby? Are
you waiting for finances and open doors to start your business or
ministry? Put those things second to getting to know the God
of your promise. As you come to know His character, first, you
will want Him more than anything. Second, you will be able to
securely rest in Him, knowing His great love for you and understanding that His plans and purposes are carried out in perfect
timing. "The riches of His glorious inheritance" will unfold to
you (Eph. 1:18, AMP).

God Is Sovereign

There comes a time in our lives when we must know and experience that God is sovereign over everything that concerns us.
Proverbs 3:1 says, "Let your heart keep my commands." If we're
going to be used by God, we must guard our hearts from attacks
of the enemy. Trusting the sovereignty of God is a heart issue.
When God is not answering us how or when we think He should,
we become perplexed and confused. Unchecked, perplexity can

cause us to become resentful and doubtful, falling into the trap of despair. Despair is an absence of hope.

When we can't figure out the whens and whys of God, our hearts can become divided. We question the integrity of God. This is why the principle in Proverbs 3:5 is important: "Trust in the LORD with *all* your heart" (emphasis added). We must be wholehearted.

Just because we are perplexed, despair does not have to follow. Second Corinthians 4:8–9 says, "We are pressured in every way [hedged in], but not crushed; perplexed [unsure of finding a way out], but not driven to despair; hunted down and persecuted, but not deserted [to stand alone]; struck down, but never destroyed" (AMP). Between your unanswered prayer and the Peninnahs, Elkanahs, and Elis, you may be carrying many of the same emotions and troubles in this season that Hannah held in hers, but hold on to hope. Do not despair. You will not be destroyed.

When we can't figure out the details of life or when the Father purposely hides many of the details of life, it is meant to draw us to seek Him. This is when we are not to lean on or be supported by our own understanding, but we are to trust His sovereignty and know that He goes before us, preparing the way for His promises not only to manifest but to take root in our lives so the fruit we produce will remain.

God Hears You

God always hears our cries. His ears are inclined to the righteous. Waiting on the Lord is not a passive activity. During times of waiting God is producing patience and endurance in our lives. These are times to focus on the Scriptures. Micah 7:7 says, "Therefore I will look unto the LORD; I will wait for the God of my salvation: my God will hear me" (KJV). I love this scripture because it clearly declares that my God will hear me. When waiting on a promise to be fulfilled, you must continually confess, "My God cares, and my God hears me." Even when it feels as if your prayers are falling on deaf ears, keep declaring, "My God hears me." Make it personal.

Do Not Grow Weary: Three Postures Hannahs Must Take

You may be feeling as if you are at the end of your rope of hope. You have been holding on as tightly as you can, but your grip is slipping. Take a deep breath, close your eyes, and hear this: You are strong. You were made to prevail over the enemy.

You may not have it all together right now, but God does. He's got you. Let His strength reposition you on your journey. Lean in to His power and let Him hold you up with His mighty right hand. Reset your focus and look to God. Restart and refresh your pursuit, knowing God is fighting for you. He hears you, and He is working it all out for your good. You are more than a conqueror, and you will have what you are praying for. As one with an anointing like Hannah's, you have a built-in measure of resistance, relentlessness, and resilience that no one else has. These three postures are setting you up for a victory you could never have imagined. Exceedingly, abundantly more than what you have asked will emerge as you claim and maintain these three positions.

1. Resistance

> So submit to [the authority of] God. Resist the devil [stand firm against him] and he will flee from you.
> —JAMES 4:7, AMP

Those of us with the Hannah anointing must learn to use the spiritual strength and authority God has given to us. Luke 10:19

says, "I give you the authority to trample on serpents and scorpions, and over all the power of the enemy, and nothing shall by any means hurt you." You are not the devil's punching bag. Resist him. Stand up to him. Shut him down. When Jesus noticed Peter was being used by Satan to get Him off focus, He called him out directly: "Get behind Me, Satan! You are a stumbling block to Me" (Matt. 16:23, AMP). We must do the same.

There was a special grace upon Hannah's life that spoke this message loud and clear, although more through actions than words. When Hannah grew tired of Peninnah's taunts, she left the area entirely and went into the presence of God. Hannah's resistance was in her ability to walk away. She demonstrated that demons were not allowed to have access to her. Hannah used Peninnah's provoking of her as a catapult to her destiny. She resisted the desire to respond to Peninnah in the flesh. Instead, she chose to win the battle on her knees. Hannah arose, went to the altar, and prayed. She allowed God to defend her.

2. Relentlessness

Don't allow fear to drive you to defeat. Hold on. The promises of God will come to pass. Stand on the promises of God. Keep going to the throne of glory. Come boldly to the throne of grace, that you may find grace to help in time of need (Heb. 4:16). Refuse to give up. You must be relentless. *Relentless* means "showing or promising no abatement of severity, intensity, strength, or pace" (*abatement* means "the act or process of reducing").[1] When you are relentless, the level of faith, confidence, motivation, and passion that you began with will be the same that you end with. You will not be moved or shaken from the place of believing God for breakthrough. You will not fade out. You will not be worn down. You will not yield, you will not relent, and you will not stop pursuing until you have all that God has promised.

This is part of the core nature of the Hannah anointing. Hannah prayed and did not lose heart until she received her promised son. God is calling all Hannahs to be courageous in the face of opposition, such as shame, impure motives, or lies of the enemy. He is calling us to be relentless until we see His promises fulfilled in our lives. We must have an unflinching confidence that even while the battle rages, we are more than conquerors through Jesus Christ (Rom. 8:37). We "must believe that [God] is, and that He is a rewarder of those who diligently seek Him" (Heb. 11:6). Don't relent until you have all that God has promised.

In the face of shame or simply being weary in well-doing, we must not lose our grip on the faithfulness of God. During these times we must tap into the unmerited grace of God. During these times of weariness we must allow our strength to come from the Lord, for God will strengthen us with might in our inner man (Eph. 3:16). He loves to see faith in His children. Hannah was a woman who, in the face of opposition, ridicule, and false accusation, kept her eye on the prize.

Hannah believed God. Hannah refused to abandon her faith. She was like a hunter in pursuit of her prey. She would not stop until she saw the goodness of God in the land of the living. Modern-day Hannahs will show no signs of slackening or yielding in their assignment from God. They will be determined, unflinching, and unyielding as they stand strong to see the promise of God fulfilled in their lives. Scripture admonishes us, "having done all, to stand" (Eph. 6:13). We must stand on the Word of the Lord.

Modern-day Hannahs will have a press in their spirit. They will press toward the goal of the high calling in Christ Jesus (Phil. 3:14). Your high call may be a son, but perhaps it's to walk in integrity with a business deal. Your upward call may be to write a book despite failing English in high school. I say to you, "Press!"

Your upward call may be to start that prayer group or get that master's or doctoral degree. Whatever the prize in Christ Jesus is for you, hear the word of the Lord: Press toward the goal! Press, and keep fighting the good fight of faith. Be relentless! Forget the voices of failure. Forget whatever the enemy is saying, such as, "It will never happen for you." The devil is a liar! Press in to Jesus until you see fruit produced in your life.

3. Resilience

> Always pray and never give up.
> —LUKE 18:1, NLT

In addition to resisting the enemy and being relentless, Hannahs are also resilient women who never give up on their God-given dreams. We have a divine ability to bounce back. We draw strength from the supply of the Spirit when faced with adversity. Modern-day Hannahs have an ability to run the race of destiny with grace. We are determined to wrestle with the promises of God in the spirit until we see them come to pass. It is not in our nature to quit at the first sign of risk or failure. We pursue the goal at hand with a steadfast, immovable heart. We face each challenge with courage and humility. We endure the pressures of life.

Second Corinthians 4:8 says, "We are hard-pressed on every side, yet not crushed." There are times in your walk with the Lord when you feel pressure—a failed or troubled marriage, a no after a job interview or for a small-business loan, or countless other challenging circumstances. We can feel crushed and want to quit when we are hard-pressed and when it seems as if we are being hit with one attack after the other from the enemy. For Hannah, it was the ridicule from her husband's other wife, being misunderstood by her husband, and being judged by the priest Eli. Those things are hard to face, and Hannah was probably feeling hard-pressed on every side, but she knew how to go to God.

The enemy will try to make you feel as if serving God is too hard. He presses and presses, squeezing tighter and tighter, hoping to choke out your passion in pursuing God and the dreams He placed in your heart. The devil crushes us with lies, telling us that we must give up or give in. The enemy wants to get you to the point where you scream out your frustration and declare, "I quit!" But he doesn't know that you hold within you the resilience, strength, and anointing that Hannah had. We must not agree with Satan by confessing that we can't go on any longer and that it is too hard. We must confess that with God all things are possible. When you are hard-pressed, you can continue to run the race with endurance. You never give up, you never give in, and you never back down. Resilience is a war weapon against the pressure to throw in the towel.

Resist the Attack of Weariness

> Lift up your tired hands, then, and strengthen your trem-
> bling knees! Keep walking on straight paths....Guard
> against turning back from the grace of God.
> —Hebrews 12:12–13, 15, GNT

The enemy of a resisting, relentless, resilient spirit is weariness. Weariness only attacks those who have been exerting strength, those who have been standing and believing over long periods of time and not seen the promise of God materialize. Many times weariness comes when we are exhausted by the toil and exertion of our own strength rather than relying on the strength of the Lord. When the enemy attacks with weariness, we must put a demand on the strength of the Lord.

Weariness opens the door for spiritual boredom, leading to

a loss of momentum. Many times you can lose the zeal of the Lord. You can even develop dullness of hearing—when you hear the promise of God but never harness the fruit of that promise. Weariness can also lead to impatience, which can cause you to make foolish and impulsive decisions. Weariness can leave you jaded, causing you to be derogatory about God, sarcastic, and facetious. You may hear yourself saying things like, "The Word of God doesn't work for me," or "I'm sick and tired of waiting on God. I'm going to just live my life." These are times when you must cling to the Word of God even more tightly. Hannah faced weariness, but she took steps to combat it. You can do the same.

Let God know how you feel.

I know it's hard when you are battling weariness, but the Lord will give you strength. When Hannah was in the midst of her season of barrenness, I am sure she was honest with the Lord as she poured out her heart. Lift up your tired hand and confess to the Lord how you're feeling. Don't put on a religious mask.

Spend time in fervent prayer.

James 5:16 says, "The effective, fervent prayer of a righteous man avails much." We see the evidence of this truth in Hannah. Though Hannah had been standing and believing for a long time, she prayed fervently, so much so that Eli thought she was drunk. Yet her fervent prayers brought about the desired result—the long-awaited fulfillment of her hopes and dreams.

When I am faced with weariness and hard-pressed by the enemy, I always stand on Jude 20, which says, "But you, beloved, build yourselves up on [the foundation of] your most holy faith [continually progress, rise like an edifice higher and higher], pray in the Holy Spirit" (AMP). You must have a revelation that you are the beloved of God—He loves you! He's not holding anything from you, and He desires to fulfill the dream He has placed in your heart.

I know I am beloved by God, so I grab hold of this verse, and I pray in the Holy Spirit. Praying in the Spirit is effective, fervent prayer that releases supernatural strength. Praying in the Spirit is a vital part of spiritual strength. It releases self-edification and builds up your faith. Weariness can weaken your faith in God, but praying in the Spirit turbocharges your faith in God and keeps you in the love of God. Romans 5:5 states, "Such hope [in God's promises] never disappoints us, because God's love has been abundantly poured out within our hearts through the Holy Spirit who was given to us" (AMP). Praying in the Spirit allows you to receive the love of God, and faith works by love (Gal. 5:6). When we understand these things, it's easy to believe and have faith in His promises to us.

Hold on to truth.

Hannah prayed for a son year after year before the Lord without an answer. She believed that she was the handmaiden of the Lord and He would cause the barren to bear. To maintain resistance, relentlessness, and resilience in the face of weariness, we must hold on to truth. The truth is God is good and He is not like man; He cannot lie. The truth of God's Word is not based on experience. Truth is based on the finished work of the cross. God has said that heaven and earth will pass away but His words will not (Matt. 24:35; Luke 21:33).

We must pray and decree the truth of God's Word over our lives. We must let the Word of God change our conditions and not let our circumstance change the word of truth. In the face of adversity and many times hopelessness, you must decree that God is and that He is a rewarder of those who seek Him (Heb. 11:6).

Hannahs have tenacious spirits that proclaim that though it may be hard, it is not impossible. Resistance, relentlessness, and resilience are inherently part of the Hannah anointing. Those who are blessed with the Hannah anointing have hearts that are strong and confident in the Lord God. No matter what the enemy does to try to stop us, we yield ourselves humbly and unwaveringly to the sovereignty and wisdom of God and His will for our lives.

Declarations Against the Spirit of Weariness

I declare that I will not lose heart or grow weary (Gal. 6:9). I will be strong in the Lord and the power of His might (Eph. 6:10).

I am a noble woman, and I will live righteously. I will not compromise my integrity to get ahead.

I will not cast away my confidence in the Lord and His promises for me (Heb. 10:35).

I will enter my due season. I will reap because I will not faint (Gal. 6:9).

I am courageous, and I have bold faith.

Having done all, I will stand (Eph. 6:13).

I will not be spiritually bored and passive.

I have the zeal of the Lord.

I have passion for God and the vision He has placed in my heart.

I will not take shortcuts or become impatient with my process. I have endurance.

I am strengthened with might in my inner man to endure and see the fulfillment of God's promises to me.

Prayers That Ignite a Relentless Spirit

Lord, Your Word says that if I believe, all things are possible (Mark 9:23). Lord, I believe. Help any area of unbelief. What man says is impossible is possible with You. I ask that You give me relentless faith. Let me see the impossible be made possible in my life. I stand on the truth of Your Word. Let the spirit of endurance rest upon me. I want to finish my course with joy, fulfillment, and fruitfulness.

I bind every intimidating force that wants to make me give up on my dream and the promises of God. I will be unyielding. I will not compromise my convictions. In the face of what is beyond my human ability, I receive Your grace. I receive the ability to do what I cannot do in my own strength. Your Word says the one who endures to the end will be saved (Matt. 24:13) and will receive what is promised (Heb. 10:36). I declare that I will not be deterred from my dream. I will press toward the goal for the prize of the upward call in Christ. I reach for Your best. I reach for Your will. I reach toward Your promises for my life. I stand on Your promises.

Remove everything that would try to distract me from the promise. Whether it's my age, time, or voices of defeat, I cast down every imagination that exalts itself against the knowledge of God. In the name of Jesus I bring every thought and argument into captivity to the obedience of Christ.

Prayers That Strengthen and Encourage While Waiting on God

Father, I thank You that You never get tired or weary. I come boldly to Your throne of glory so You will give

*me supernatural strength. Lord, give me power to over-
come this weakness. I ask that You will increase my
strength. I wait on You, and my strength is renewed. I
am strengthened with might in my inner man. The joy
of the Lord is my strength. I am strong in You and in
the power of Your might. I declare You are my strength.
You will make my feet like hinds' feet, and I will walk
upon the high hills of life. Your way, O Lord, is strength
for the upright. You are my refuge and strength, a very
present help in a time of trouble. I declare that I can do
all things through Christ who strengthens me. I wait for
You, Lord. I will be strong and take courage.*

Prayers and Declarations for Persisting in Prayer

*I declare that I won't give up or give in. I will not sur-
render my faith in the promises of God. I ask, seek, and
knock, and the doors of promise will be opened to me.
I will seek Your face continually. Lord, I ask that You
will release the spirit of perseverance over my life. Holy
Spirit, teach me to persist in prayer. Let the spirit of
prayer rest upon my life. Let me be on alert; quicken my
spirit to press in to Your kingdom. I break the spirit of
slumber off of my life. I break the spirit of the sloth off
of my life. I will be diligent in prayer. Let the force of
intercession rest upon my life. I decree that the ability to
pray effective, fervent prayers will rest on my life. I am
God's battle-ax, His weapon of war. I am His battering
ram in the spirit. I pray at all times in the Spirit. I will
not cease to pray. The spirit of grace and supplication is
upon my life.*

Chapter 4

THE REMEDY

Search me [thoroughly], O God, and know my heart; test me
and know my anxious thoughts; and see if there is any wicked
or hurtful way in me, and lead me in the everlasting way.
—PSALM 139:23–24, AMP

COUPLES WHO HAVE unsuccessfully tried for a baby through natural means know well the process doctors go through to figure out
whose physiology is keeping them from reaching their dreams of
being parents. In the case of Hannah and Elkanah, Hannah was
the barren one. Nothing was wrong with her husband, as he was
able to have children with his other wife, Peninnah. Knowing
she was the one limited in this area must have added to Hannah's despair.

When she married a man who loved her and showed her favor,
Hannah must have thought she was on her way to having the
family of her dreams. But then it happened—nothing. Nothing
happened. After trying and trying, and seeing the other wife have
child after child, Hannah had nothing. She had no child. She did
not conceive the son she dreamed of and prayed for. What had
she done wrong? How had she fallen out of favor with God?

Perhaps your barrenness, or infertility, after doing all the
right things is the very thing that leads you to identify so closely
with Hannah. You see everyone around you with babies or businesses. You see them thriving. There's fruitfulness all around
except with you.

Allow me to comfort you with this: this is a season that will soon pass. Just as God heard the prayer of Hannah and delivered to her the promised son, God will deliver His promise to you. In this difficult time you can trust that God will use your circumstances to bring about His eternal plan. I believe Hannah encountered God in an unusual way in her season of heartache and pain. He revealed things about Himself to Hannah as she continually drew near to the Lord. At the end of her testing and trial she prophesied and declared wisdom and revelation never mentioned before in Scripture. For example, she spoke of inheriting a throne of glory (1 Sam. 2:8). I believe she spent time around this throne of glory, beholding the beauty of the Lord. When she declared that no one was like God (1 Sam. 2:2), they weren't empty words—she had a personal encounter with the Lord, the kind of encounter the Lord wants with all of us.

Just as Hannah did, I want you to profit from your pain. Take your setbacks, disappointments, and lack of understanding to the throne of glory. There is something bigger going on in your life. God will shape your heart to understand His perspective of your life. Take advantage of God's focus on your heart during this time. He is preparing it to grow and nurture the seed He will soon deliver. Let Him show you any unholy things hiding in your heart. Make these verses your prayer during this season:

> Create in me a clean heart, O God, and renew a right and steadfast spirit within me. Do not cast me away from Your presence and do not take Your Holy Spirit from me. Restore to me the joy of Your salvation and sustain me with a willing spirit.
>
> —PSALM 51:10–12, AMP

Hannah prayed year after year for a son, but it wasn't until her prayers changed and she made a new vow to God that she received what was promised.

Getting Back on the Right Road

You are moving quickly toward a season of upgrade. You will not be where you are forever. I've learned that whenever I feel as if I missed the mark in my journey to fulfill my destiny, I need to incorporate repentance in my prayer time. Nothing takes the place of repentance. The wrong road does not become the right road until you turn around and go back to where you were before you took the wrong turn.

When we are on the wrong road, humility is important. The sooner we recognize we've made a wrong turn, the sooner we can repent and get back on the right road. Repentance leads you back to the right path. We can say, "Father, I repent. Lead me in the way everlasting."

Repentance is one of the major ways we get spiritual break-through. My mentor told me, "Michelle, you have to align your life with the Word of God. You must come to a place where you understand the Word." When we are gifted, we don't always know when we are in error because our gifts still work. Romans 11:29 says, "For the gifts and the calling of God are irrevocable [for He does not withdraw what He has given, nor does He change His mind about those to whom He gives His grace or to whom He sends His call]" (AMP). This means you can walk and move in the things of God and still be out of the will of God. This barren season should be a time of deep reflection and self-examination. It's a time when the Lord is very close to you, pulling at your heart. He desires to encounter you, but He needs your undivided attention.

Think about this: Jesus said that at the end of time there will be people who say, "Lord, Lord, have we not prophesied in Your name?" (Matt. 7:22). Jesus will respond, "I never knew you; depart from Me" (v. 23). These people were recognized for being accurate in their prophecies, but accuracy doesn't mean you are in the will of God. The will of God is about walking true to your purpose. It's about what you do in the secret place. Paul wrote, "But I discipline my body and keep it under control, lest after preaching to others I myself should be disqualified" (1 Cor. 9:27, ESV). If you have a life that aligns with God, then you will see breakthroughs.

Bind Up the Little Foxes

Could it be that you are not seeing breakthrough and fruitfulness in your life because your character needs an alignment? Sometimes we hunger after the wrong things. We want to be in leadership and be known as prophets, prophetesses, apostles, pastors, or this or that, but those positions will pass away. But the fruit that God imparts to us—the fruit of the Spirit—will remain. He chose us for this very thing. He says, "You did not choose Me, but I chose you and appointed you that you should go and bear fruit, and that your fruit should remain, that whatever you ask the Father in My name He may give you" (John 15:16).

God didn't choose you to just exist and to live a life with no fruit. Therefore, it is important to confront and eliminate hindrances that get in the way of your fruitfulness. Such hindrances might include erroneous mind-sets, soul ties, a poor self-image, pride, blame shifting, self-justification, or people pleasing.

Though we have demonic forces coming against us, some of the hindrances that cause the most damage come from within. They are like the little foxes that spoil the vine (Song of Sol. 2:15). They gnaw and chew on the vine, spoiling your harvest. Pray that the fire of the Holy Ghost will burn up any little foxes—any little vice, demonic fox, relationship, or mind-set—spoiling your fruit.

As a man thinks in his heart, so is he (Prov. 23:7). Break destructive and erroneous thinking, and think as God thinks. "Be renewed in the spirit of your mind" (Eph. 4:23), and see yourself as God sees you. See yourself as prosperous and moving forward.

Also, watch your words. Gossip will eat up our harvest. Words of death or disbelief have the power to render your seed lifeless. Let words of life and faith come forth out of your mouth. Rebuke and shut down any lying spirits.

Be bold and repent of anything that is stopping your fruitfulness. Cast out anything that is not like God. If you don't know what it is, ask God. Whatever little foxes are spoiling your vines, you must let the Lord deliver you from them all. No vice is worth holding on to at the expense of not bearing much fruit.

Heart issues can be hidden from the world sometimes, but we cannot hide them from God. God loves us too much to leave us in our place of ignorance, error, or faulty thinking. He can heal our hearts and bring us back into alignment with His will so it can come to fruition in our lives. God wants to make our hearts and minds ready for the breakthrough that will surely come.

A breakthrough is "a sudden increase in knowledge, understanding, etc.: an important discovery that happens after trying for a long time to understand or explain something." It is also "a sudden advance or successful development."[1] I am decreeing that your heart will be ready for God to suddenly advance, enhance, refine, and improve your life so you will be positioned for breakthrough. May you have a sudden increase in knowledge and understanding concerning your destiny and the will of God for your life. No matter what the devil is throwing at you, you are in a season when you must stand on the Word of God and remain in the center of God's will.

Remain in the Vine

> I am the vine, you are the branches. He who abides in
> Me, and I in him, bears much fruit; for without Me you
> can do nothing.
>
> —JOHN 15:5

For our hearts to be one with God's concerning His promise to us, we have to abide in Him. *Abide* means to remain, stay, dwell, endure, or continue to be present.[2] Jesus is telling us that if we remain in Him and continue to be present with Him, we will bear much fruit. He is the vine, and as branches we cannot survive separate from Him.

In my book *The Anna Anointing*, I talk about what it means to abide (*meno* in Greek) in Christ:

> *Abide* is the Greek word *meno*, meaning "to stay, to remain, to continue, or to permanently abide in one place." The word *meno* gives the idea that something is rooted, unmoving, and steadfast. We learn to abide in Christ by applying the Word of God to our everyday lives. We must look obediently to His Word as the final authority in our lives. We must apply His promises to our hearts. Our hearts and desires are transformed into a life that bears fruit.[3]

Notice the definition of *abide* says "to permanently abide in one place." Consider the place Hannah poured out her desires to the Lord, the place she went when things at home were too much to bear. Hannah made the sanctuary, the temple of the Lord, her abode. She abided in the presence of God. If you want breakthrough, abide in the presence of God.

Beloved, the entirety of your life matters to God. You may feel as if He is not listening or doesn't care because this barren season has continued long without a breakthrough. But be sure of this: God is faithful. He will complete the work He is doing as you wait for your Samuel. He loves you and wants to see you produce, multiply, and replenish the earth. But just as God wanted to communicate with His people all those years before Samuel was born because He loves to share His secrets with His servants, there were also some things God was not going to overlook. His people needed to come back in line and in fellowship and in agreement with Him. They needed to repent of turning their backs on Him and worshipping other gods. There were also things Hannah had to come to agreement with. She prayed:

> O LORD of hosts, if You will indeed look on the affliction (suffering) of Your maidservant and remember, and not forget Your maidservant, but will give Your maidservant a son, then I will give him to the LORD all the days of his life; a razor shall never touch his head.
> —1 SAMUEL 1:11, AMP

Once Hannah made this vow, she solidified to herself and God her commitment to dedicate the fulfillment of her promise to God for holy use. Then when the appointed time came, Hannah conceived and bore a son. She spent time with God. She endured and remained in Him and was able to come to understand His will for her and the seed she so desired to birth.

Daughter, your appointed time has come. Get in the presence of God so He may impart to you His plan to usher you to a time of breakthrough and fruitfulness. Jesus said that if you abide in Him and His Word abides in you, you can ask what you will, and it will be given to you (John 15:7). The secret to breaking seasons of barrenness is twofold: repentance and abiding in Christ. As you focus your prayers and absorb the insights as the Lord gives you revelation, you will see fruitfulness, blessing, and increase. I pray that you will see these days turn into seasons of multiplication. Don't let the enemy stop you. Repent and abide in the Lord, and bear much fruit.

Abide in Christ

The enemy works overtime to make the simple act of abiding in Christ more mysterious and abstract than it actually is. Depending on where you are in your walk with God, the concept of abiding in Christ can sound ungraspable, so let me demystify it for you. Abiding in Christ is centered on your communication with Him through prayer, worship, and reading and obeying His Word.

Prayer

Talk to Jesus. We have to talk to God about what we want, who we are, and where we want to see the fruit of God manifest in our lives. We have to break out of the frenzy in the body of Christ concerning our ability to hear the word of the Lord. There is such anxiety about knowing what God is saying. We have to pull ourselves away from the madness and really center in on Jesus. Take fifteen minutes right after you read this chapter, and just talk to Jesus.

Realize that Jesus sent the Comforter—the Holy Spirit—who now lives inside you, walking with you, teaching you, and guiding you, and He will share the secrets of the kingdom with you if you seek Him and ask. Set aside some time to commune with Jesus. The devil will taunt you by saying you look foolish and that you are talking to yourself. But we have an audience with the King. Because of Jesus we can boldly approach the throne.

Talk to Jesus. Talk to God. Commune with the Spirit of God. God doesn't want us to serve Him in blind obedience. He says, "Come now, and let us reason together" (Isa. 1:18). You can tell God, "I really don't understand this. My flesh won't submit in this area. Please help me. I want to do Your will. Teach me. Show me," and He will honor the purity of your heart. Being authentic with God and watching Him respond with help from on high builds strong faith.

When you have an honest relationship with God, you can talk openly with Him and know that He hears you, and He can talk openly to you, and you will hear Him. Whenever I come to this concept, I think about the greatest God-human relationships. None of the humans were perfect, but they all had a strong bond with God because they were honest with Him and submitted to His lordship. Consider Moses, David, Job, and, of course, Hannah. They did not hide their fears, weaknesses, longings, or wants. God knew it all. Look at the breakthroughs, victories, and deliverances they experienced. I encourage you to meditate on their lives, knowing that you can abide in God at an even greater level than they did, for they did not have the Holy Spirit living inside them.

Worship

Worship is an instrument of prayer. Worship brings us face to face and into close contact with God. Hannah surrendered her most valued possession to the Lord—her dream! There comes a time when you have to give God the glory due His name. Take the names of God and proclaim them out loud. Lift God up over your situation. *Worship* literally means to make yourself low. Spend some time bowing down and kneeling as an act of surrender. Ask the Lord how you can serve Him. Don't ask Him for anything during this time; just minister to Him.

Reading and obeying His Word

We need to read the Word, apply God's promises, and submit to His leadership. We apply the Word of God to our hearts by confessing the truth of the Word and resisting the lies of the

enemy. Reading the Word out loud and then asking the Holy
Spirit for understanding causes faith to arise in our hearts. The
Word becomes what I call living understanding, or understanding
that lives in your heart, making it easy to apply and live by. You
are transformed from just hearing the Word, and faith arises for
you to become a doer of the Word. "Take words with you, and
return to the LORD. Say to Him, 'Take away all iniquity; receive
us graciously, for we will offer the sacrifices of our lips" (Hos.
14:2). The prophet admonishes us to take words with us as we
encounter the presence of the Lord. The words we should take
back to God are the words of the Bible. Speaking them back to
Him will open up new insight and wisdom from His heart. You
will think like Him and see things by the Spirit regarding your
life and destiny.

There is no greater way to show God you trust Him and
love Him than by obeying Him. It is greater than sacrifice and
worship.

> Has the LORD as great a delight in burnt offerings and
> sacrifices as in obedience to the voice of the LORD?
> Behold, to obey is better than sacrifice, and to heed [is
> better] than the fat of rams. For rebellion is as [serious
> as] the sin of divination (fortune-telling), and disobedi-
> ence is as [serious as] false religion and idolatry.
> —1 SAMUEL 15:22–23, AMP

As a matter of fact, obedience is an act of worship. Presenting
ourselves before God in a way that is holy and pleasing to Him
is our reasonable act of worship (Rom. 12:1). We confirm our love
for God by obeying Him. Jesus said, "If you love Me, keep My
commandments" (John 14:15). Disobedience separates you from
God. Obedience draws you near.

Like a Table Set Before You

The Lord gave me a picture of a table—His table—and we, the saints of God, are seated at it. The table is overflowing with fruit of all kinds, and we are invited to eat until we are full. He is inviting us to partake of the fruit of His labor. God doesn't want us to keep working in the field, planting seed, and watering it without ever seeing the harvest.

I believe God is inviting you into the next season. You are seeking and abiding in Him even in the winter season, but harvesttime is coming. Let the harvest of the Lord come.

The Bible talks about seedtime and harvest. We have sown through tears and prayers and fasting; it is now time to harvest the fruit of that seed. Psalm 126:5–6 says, "They who sow in tears shall reap with joyful singing. He who goes back and forth weeping, carrying his bag of seed [for planting], will indeed come again with a shout of joy, bringing his sheaves with him" (AMP).

Woman of God, it is your harvest season. The Lord has prepared a table before you in the presence of your enemies. He is inviting you into your season of abundance, manifestation, and overflow. May you receive more than what you've asked for. May God exceed your expectations.

Once you get what you've asked for, it's not over. God wants you to be free to give out what you have been given. That you have been blessed to be a blessing is an important part of reproducing fruit that remains. You were discipled by God, and now you become one who disciples others. What you have you give. What you have belongs to God; it is not yours.

Isaiah 54 is God's declaration to the barren ones who will give birth according to His plan. Some Hannahs will have spiritual sons and daughters who will be more in number than their natural children. Just as Hannah had to adjust her expectations regarding her promised son, you may have to make a new vow according to God's will for your life. I encourage you to declare this prophetic word over yourself in faith even as you wait. God will surely deliver on all His promises.

> "Sing, O barren, you who have not borne! Break forth into singing, and cry aloud, you who have not labored with child! For more are the children of the desolate than the children of the married woman," says the LORD. "Enlarge the place of your tent, and let them stretch out the curtains of your dwellings; do not spare; lengthen your cords, and strengthen your stakes. For you shall expand to the right and to the left, and your descendants will inherit the nations, and make the desolate cities inhabited. Do not fear, for you will not be ashamed; neither be disgraced, for you will not be put to shame; for you will forget the shame of your youth."
> —ISAIAH 54:1–4

This is your season for expansion. You will sing. You will prophesy. You will decree. Growth, abundance, multiplication, prosperity, and overflow are coming to your house. No more scarcity and lack. The Lord is your Shepherd; you shall not want (Ps. 23:1). The Spirit of God is searching your heart to find anything that is not like God, any hindrances that stand in your way. He will make you clean. He will heal you—mind, body, and spirit— and cause you to bear fruit that remains.

Prayers That Come Against a Victim Mind-Set

I decree I am not a victim; I am a victor through Christ Jesus. I bind every lying and seducing spirit that makes me think everyone is against me. I am not help- less or hopeless. I believe God. I cannot always control what happens to me, but I can control how I respond. I decree I will not have a distorted perspective or limited thinking. My identity will not be rooted in what has happened to me. I will be made whole. I will bear children. I will be fruitful and multiply. I will not live as a victim. I will not live with doubt and unbelief. My barrenness is not a member of my family. I will not nurse it or justify it. It is not my future. I will be renewed in the spirit of my mind. Thanks be unto God, who gives me the victory through Jesus Christ!

Prayers That Come Against Poor Self-Image

I choose to look outwardly instead of focusing on myself. I rebuke every feeling of inadequacy. Lord, You are the potter, and I am the clay. I am Your vessel of honor. I cast down every imagination that says I am not good enough, I am not smart enough, or my body is broken. I decree that I am fearfully and wonderfully made. I loose myself from all spirits of self-hatred. I am beautiful. I am strong. I can do all things through Christ, who strengthens me. I rebuke and silence every inner voice that tells me I'm not good enough to have a child or I am not strong enough to run a company. I decree that I am worthy of love. I thank You, Lord, that I am Your handiwork, Your masterpiece.

Prayer of Repentance

Father, create in me a clean heart and renew a righteous spirit within me. Lord, forgive me for staggering. I lay aside every weight and sin that easily ensnares me. I loose myself from carrying the weight of my promise being fulfilled. I cast this care on You. I look to You, Jesus, the author and finisher of my faith. I will trust You with my dream and receive Your grace to run this race. I will fulfill my destiny by Your Spirit, not by my effort. I repent for trying to expedite Your process. My times are in Your hands. Purify my heart, purify my motives, and remove wrong thinking. Let me be renewed in the spirit of my mind. I cast down every imagination and argument that exalts itself against You. I repent for allowing anxiety and fear of the future to rule in my heart. I repent of doubt and unbelief. Cleanse me from the evil heart of doubt. I choose to believe You. I repent of pride and self-righteousness. Take out my hardness of heart, and give me a heart of flesh. I trust You with all my heart and lean not on my own understanding.

Chapter 5

THE ENEMIES THAT GATHER

> Peninnah had children, but Hannah had none....Hannah's rival provoked her bitterly, to irritate and embarrass her, because the LORD had left her childless. So it happened year after year, whenever she went up to the house of the LORD, Peninnah provoked her; so she wept and would not eat.
>
> —1 Samuel 1:2, 6–7, AMP

EVEN AS YOU overcome the internal hindrances that come against the fulfillment of God's promises, there are enemies coming against you from the outside. These enemies include jealousy, compromise, misunderstanding, judgment, and criticism. In the life of Hannah we can see these characteristics personified in Peninnah, Elkanah, and Eli, three of the people who were closest to Hannah as she battled through barrenness and infertility.

Weariness can lead you to give in to these enemies. Jealousy from others may cause you to want to shrink back and diminish the intensity of your pursuit. You may feel as if you want to make yourself smaller so people won't mistake your confidence and optimism for arrogance. A spirit of jealousy could also be transferred to you as you see others receive the kind of breakthrough and blessing you've been praying for. Compromise may cause you to feel as if you have set your hopes too high and you don't deserve all you are praying for. With misunderstanding, judgment, and criticism, you may be led to doubt what you heard from God or to believe that maybe it doesn't take all that praying, worshipping, and fasting to see your dreams become reality.

These outside enemies are sent to do the same thing the inside enemies attempt to do: make you quit and miss out on the promise of God being fulfilled in your life. They come to steal, kill, and destroy the fruit of your dream before it is birthed. But rest assured, not one of the weapons the enemy forms against you will prosper. You have come this far by faith, and God is going to see you through to the other side. He says:

> Indeed they shall surely assemble, but not because of Me. Whoever assembles against you shall fall for your sake....No weapon formed against you shall prosper, and every tongue which rises against you in judgment you shall condemn. This is the heritage of the servants of the LORD, and their righteousness is from Me.
> —ISAIAH 54:15, 17

We are going to look at these enemies, identifying their tactics and examining how Hannah's grace, humility, and unyielding focus helped her gain the victory over each of these enemies and, in one case, turned an enemy into an ally.

Peninnah and the Enemy of Jealousy

Jealousy is one of those behaviors that Christians don't call out as much as some other sins, such as sexual immorality. But jealousy is as much a sin as unfaithfulness to a husband or wife. Jealousy is clearly an ungodly and destructive behavior, and God does not like it.

Jealousy is hostility toward a rival or someone believed to have an advantage.[1] Jealousy leads a person to treat the target of her jealousy with great resistance and opposition. This person is unfriendly, antagonistic, and offensive. Covetousness and envy are companion behaviors that go right along with jealousy. Covetousness is "marked by inordinate desire for wealth or possessions or for another's possessions," while envy is a "painful or resentful awareness of an advantage enjoyed by another joined with a desire to possess the same advantage."[2] Jealous people are keenly aware that they lack something, but instead of working hard for it or going to God about it, their brokenness leads them to torment, taunt, and grieve others who have what they think they should have.

Have you ever been the victim of jealousy? Has someone just had it out for you, your position, or your anointing? Has anyone ever competed with you in a game you didn't know you were playing? If so, then you know how perplexing and destructive it is to oneself and to others:

> Surely vexation kills the fool, and jealousy slays the simple.
>
> —JOB 5:2, ESV

> A heart at peace gives life to the body, but envy rots the bones.
>
> —PROVERBS 14:30, NIV

> Anger is cruel and fury overwhelming, but who can stand before jealousy?
>
> —PROVERBS 27:4, NIV

Another version of Proverbs 27:4 says, "Who is able to endure and stand before [the sin of] jealousy?" (AMP). Jealousy can be all-consuming for both the victim and the perpetrator. If victims do not sever ties with a jealous person, they can be overtaken by it as the good things life brings them are suffocated. The perpetrator will be consumed by jealousy's insatiable and everlasting fire. A jealous person's desires cannot be satisfied. A jealous person also cannot be reasoned with, because her mentality is stuck on entitlement and based on insecurity that can only be healed in the presence of God.

Jealousy is worldly and carnal:

> You are still worldly {carnal, NKJV} [controlled by ordinary impulses, the sinful capacity]. For as long as there is jealousy and strife and discord among you, are you not unspiritual, and are you not walking like ordinary men [unchanged by faith]?
> —1 CORINTHIANS 3:3, AMP

Jealousy is evil and demonic and opens the door to all kinds of sinful and base practices:

> But if you have bitter jealousy and selfish ambition in your hearts, do not be arrogant, and [as a result] be in defiance of the truth. This [superficial] wisdom is not that which comes down from above, but is earthly (secular), natural (unspiritual), even demonic. For where jealousy and selfish ambition exist, there is disorder [unrest, rebellion] and every evil thing and morally degrading practice.
> —JAMES 3:14–16, AMP

Jealousy is a work of the flesh:

> Now the works of the flesh are evident: sexual immorality, impurity, sensuality, idolatry, sorcery, enmity, strife, *jealousy*, fits of anger, rivalries, dissensions, divisions, *envy*, drunkenness, orgies, and things like these.

I warn you, as I warned you before, that those who do such things will not inherit the kingdom of God.
—Galatians 5:19–21, esv, emphasis added

Jealousy takes root where there is no love:

Love is patient, love is kind. It does not envy, it does not boast, it is not proud.
—1 Corinthians 13:4, niv

Jealousy is indicative of emotional or spiritual pain or emptiness. It has roots in fear (fear of not having or being enough, or fear of rejection for not being or having enough), anger, resentment, and bitterness at God or "life" because of not getting what one thinks is deserved. Jealous people are insecure, and they reject good things because they were rejected at some point. They desperately need love and affirmation, though they reject it when it comes.

In Hannah's story Peninnah is the jealous antagonist. We assume she was jealous because her husband loved Hannah more and gave Hannah a double portion of the sacrificial meat, even though Hannah had no children.

When the day came that Elkanah sacrificed, he would give portions [of the sacrificial meat] to Peninnah his wife and all her sons and daughters. But to Hannah he would give a double portion, because he loved Hannah, but the Lord had given her no children.
—1 Samuel 1:4–5, amp

Peninnah was in pain even though she had children. She was lacking in a significant area of her life—the need to be cherished and loved by her husband. All her children were not a substitute for the love and acceptance she needed from her husband, but even more so from God. I imagine her prayers may have been more like complaints: "Why won't he look at me the way he does Hannah? Why won't he love me as he loves her? Why can't I have a double portion? I've given him a quiver full of children. Hannah has given him none. It's not fair. God, I want what she has."

This is not the way to go to God. Because of what the Scriptures show us about jealousy, we can conclude that Peninnah did not have a close relationship with God. She did not go to Him with her desires in order to have them purified or to have anything cast out that hindered her from having what she truly needed. She did not listen for what God specifically and uniquely planned for her to bring her the fulfillment she desired. Instead, she went after what Hannah had: "You covet but you cannot get what you want, so you quarrel and fight. You do not have because you do not ask God. When you ask, you do not receive, because you ask with wrong motives, that you may spend what you get on your pleasures" (Jas. 4:2–3, NIV).

Peninnah wanted love, but she wasn't loving or lovable. She was treacherous and mean. Day after day she teased, taunted, and provoked Hannah until Hannah came to tears and could not eat. The Bible calls Peninnah an adversary and rival. The Hebrew word for *adversary* is *tsarah*, and it means "adversity, affliction, anguish, distress, tribulation, trouble." It means "vexer" or "rival wife."[3] An adversary is "one that contends with, opposes, or resists: an enemy or opponent."[4] A rival is "one of two or more striving to reach or obtain something that only one can possess; one striving for competitive advantage." *Rival* also means "to be in competition with." Rivals also seek to emulate, equal, or excel over another. Synonyms include "challenger" and "competitor."[5] As Hannah's rival and adversary, Peninnah provoked Hannah, never letting her forget that God had not given her children. The Hebrew word for *provoke* means to anger, to vex, to trouble, to grieve, to have sorrow, to irritate.[6]

From the definitions listed, it looks as if jealous words and actions are right in line with what some call verbal or emotional abuse and others call bullying—a concerning topic. People lose hope and the desire to live because of vicious attacks from vexing, demonic, and evil people. Words hurt just as much as, and maybe more than, physical violence. Relentless taunting and teasing causes some people to struggle with deep depression, anxiety, insecurity, and thoughts of suicide and worthlessness. When we are victims of the spirit of jealousy, it attacks our self-worth.

Psalm 43:5 reads, "Why are you cast down, O my soul? And why are you disquieted within me? Hope in God; for I shall yet praise Him, the help of my countenance and my God." Verbal attacks have a way of bringing us to a place of despair. It is a place we go to when the light of hope has been put out. We feel as if we cannot look up with hope and expectancy for fear of being teased for even being positive.

Teasing, taunts, and bullying have a diabolical way of attacking our identity, who we are. But they are full of lies. If we don't know what God has spoken over us, we will be in the fight of our lives against the destructive force behind jealousy. Jealousy's lies cause us to fret. Peninnah "provoked [Hannah] sore, for to make her fret" (1 Sam. 1:6, kjv). Fretting is an enemy against Hannahs during the season of waiting and preparation, as I discussed in chapter 2. Fretting gets your eyes off of God and onto your own situation.

Peninnah was being purposefully used by the enemy. The enemy loves division and contention. Peninnah had children of her own, yet she still wanted what Hannah had. But you cannot satisfy a jealous person by giving her what you have. That evil spirit will continue to cry out for more until you have nothing left. This is why you cannot give place to the spirit of jealousy. It must be cast out. You cannot occupy the same space as a person who is jealous of you. She will never rest until she sees you come to nothing.

Hannah was not willing to give up what God had for her. Her strategy was to stay away from Peninnah and remain in the presence of God, where she could hear over and over again who she was in Him. She dwelled in the presence of God because He affirmed her identity. There is no record of Hannah responding verbally to Peninnah. Instead, she got up from the table to go to the sanctuary of the Lord.

Too often women compete with one another for things that are equally available to all. Other times we want something that is special or unique to another woman, not accepting and pursuing our own uniqueness that enables us to shine. But Hannahs cannot afford ungodly competition. It destroys the grace and humility that is central to our identity. It creates ungodly distractions and gets our focus and eyes off of God. We also cannot get caught up in trying to figure out why someone is jealous of us—that is truly between that person and God. Instead, quietly dismiss yourself from the person's table and get to the house of God, your prayer closet, or whatever place you've set apart for your time with God.

Turn the Other Cheek

One of the most effective ways to overcome the spirit of jealousy is by practicing Jesus' command to turn the other cheek. Now, before you think this means to allow yourself to get smacked in the face by your enemies once, then turn the other cheek to them so they can do it again, let me share this revelation with you. Jesus' command is really about our keeping our faces centered on the promise—not turning our faces to the left or the right but staying focused and letting God defend us.

> But I say to you, do not resist an evil person [who insults you or violates your rights]; but whoever slaps you on the right cheek, turn the other toward him also [simply ignore insignificant insults or trivial losses and do not bother to retaliate—maintain your dignity, your self-respect, your poise].
>
> —MATTHEW 5:39, AMP

As we saw, Hannah did not say or do anything to Peninnah. She kept her mind and heart focused on God. Hannah set her face like flint and trusted that the Lord would keep her from being put to shame. (See Isaiah 50:7.) When the enemy attacked her, she turned her face toward God. When we have the same understanding, we can declare:

+ "I've got my eye on the goal, where God is beckoning [me] onward....I'm off and running, and I'm not turning back." So I keep focused on that goal, because I want everything God has for me (Phil. 3:12–16, MSG).

+ Because I have focused my love on God, I know He will deliver me. He will protect me because He knows my name. When I call out to Him, He will answer me. God is with me in my distress. He will deliver me, and He will honor me. (See Psalm 91:14–15.)

+ "How I love you, LORD! You are my defender. The LORD is my protector; he is my strong fortress. My God is my protection, and with him I am safe. He protects me like a shield; he defends me and keeps me safe" (Ps. 18:1–2, GNT).

Hannah knew the importance of keeping her focus on God. She did not lose her mind under the abuse and ridicule Peninnah launched her way. Isaiah 26:3 says, "You will keep in perfect and constant peace the one whose mind is steadfast [that is, committed and focused on You—in both inclination and character], because he trusts and takes refuge in You [with hope and confident expectation]" (AMP).

Don't Be a Peninnah

Jealousy and bitterness have a way of keeping you in seasons of barrenness for too long. In some ways Peninnah carried a spirit that is like the counter-anointing for the Hannah anointing. Peninnah took time and energy away from caring for her children and spent it on bullying and abusing Hannah. She was distracted by her efforts to make Hannah's life miserable. Hannah was focused; Peninnah was divided. Hannah was fruitful in the spirit; Peninnah was lacking and empty.

How do we respond when we don't have what we think we should? Can we support and cheer other women and their success while we wait for our own? Do we respond with jealousy, unable to see and enjoy what we do have? When you are busy looking at another woman's progress and envying her, you miss out on the lessons and private time with God that will lead you to the breakthrough you've been pursuing.

Jealousy causes us to forget what we have already. Jealousy causes us to underappreciate the benefits, privileges, and blessings we have and overvalue the possessions of others. "Jealousy can turn life into a competition about who has the best, is the best, and can show off the most. This attitude pleases the god of this world (Satan), not the true God....Jealousy continually whispers to us, 'God's gifts are not good enough. You need/ deserve/should have whatever you want in this life.'"[7]

Thankfulness and contentment go a long way in helping us keep our focus on our own journey. Being thankful for what God has done in your own life is very important as you see others prosper. Thankfulness also keeps you focused on where God has brought you from. Thankfulness keeps you in the moment, while jealousy gets you thinking too far ahead.

Hannahs hold a special place in God's heart. There is no reason for us to be jealous:

> Do not worry because of evildoers, nor be envious toward wrongdoers; for they will wither quickly like the grass, and fade like the green herb. Trust [rely on and have confidence] in the LORD and do good; dwell in the land and feed [securely] on His faithfulness. Delight yourself in the LORD, and He will give you the desires and petitions of your heart.
> —PSALM 37:1–4, AMP

Elkanah—Don't Compromise; Contend for the Promise

> Her husband Elkanah would say to her, "Hannah, why are you weeping? Why don't you eat? Why are you downhearted? Don't I mean more to you than ten sons?"
> —1 SAMUEL 1:8, NIV

We know they mean well, but husbands cannot take the place of God's promise coming to pass in our lives. So let's get one thing straight: there are no consolation prizes in the kingdom of God. If the Lord gave you a promise or dream, don't settle for anything else or anything less than what He promised you.

Hannah's husband was clueless to cries of Hannah's heart. Hannah didn't want ten sons—she wanted the one God promised her. Elkanah's questions presented her with a compromise she was not willing to take. Her response is in her actions. When she chose to return to the sanctuary to pray, she was telling her husband, "No, you cannot take the place of God's promise to me. I will not forget the longing to bear this son. I will not stop crying out to God. I will not stop fasting. I want all that God has promised me, and I will not settle for anything else."

When the Lord has chosen you as a forerunner to birth and advance His promise in the earth, it can be a very lonely time in your life. Often the people closest to you will misunderstand your passion and zeal to see the dream fulfilled. Elkanah's questions reveal his patronizing heart toward his wife and just how clueless he was to the pain he caused by bringing another woman into the house. Scripture does not reveal why Elkanah did not stand in faith with Hannah to believe God for a son. He succumbed to the pressures of the culture and obtained a second wife to perpetuate his legacy.

The spirit of compromise can subtly seep into your heart. You must understand how important your work is to God. It may seem small in man's eyes, but your dream, your vision, or the birth of your child is important in the eyes of God.

According to the *Collins Dictionary*, "a compromise is a situation in which people accept something slightly different from what they really want, because of circumstances or because they are considering the wishes of other people; if you compromise with someone, you reach an agreement with them in which you both give up something that you originally wanted."[8] If you're like me, compromise doesn't sound good at all. We must resolve to never give in to compromise and never settle for less than what the Lord has promised us. Elkanah's question was subtly laced in compromise. It insinuated that she should settle on him being enough for her. The compromise was like a vapor seeping in underneath the door. Hannahs must be adamant about what we believe God has promised us and be ready to fight to fulfillment and to victory.

While waiting on the promise of God, you may be faced with doubt and unbelief. You have to overcome the pressure to doubt the goodness of God. One of David's declarations was "I would have lost heart, unless I had believed that I would see the goodness of the LORD in the land of the living" (Ps. 27:13). In times of waiting on a promise, you are forced to dig deep to see who you really are and what you truly believe. When the opportunity comes to compromise or settle for less than what God promised, just say no. Wait patiently on God, and He will strengthen your resolve. Tell the enemy, "I will not be shaken. I will not be moved. I will keep my eyes on God and all He has for me." Stand on the promise. Stay faithful to the course.

Eli: Destiny Partners—From Misjudgment to Agreement

> Now it happened as she continued praying before the LORD, that Eli was watching her mouth. Hannah was speaking in her heart (mind); only her lips were moving, and her voice was not heard, so Eli thought she was drunk. Eli said to her, "How long will you make yourself drunk? Get rid of your wine."
>
> —1 SAMUEL 1:12–14, AMP

No one likes to be judged. Eli misjudged Hannah and spoke to her in a religiously condescending way, but Hannah had the wisdom and grace to turn the situation around in her favor. She gently corrected him and established the truth: "No, my lord, I am a woman with a despairing spirit. I have not been drinking wine or any intoxicating drink, but I have poured out my soul before the LORD" (v. 15). Then she requested that he adjust his view and empathize with her situation: "Do not regard your maidservant as a wicked and worthless woman, for I have spoken until now out of my great concern and [bitter] provocation" (v. 16). She pulled on the compassion of the man of God. Because of his prophetic nature Eli was able to discern her sincerity, so he released and spoke a blessing over her that was the final ingredient to break Hannah's season of barrenness. He said, "Go in peace; and may the God of Israel grant your petition that you have asked of Him" (v. 17). In an instant Hannah received the full measure of her name. Grace and favor found her. Her countenance lifted. The Bible says she was no longer sad (v. 18).

There comes a point when we can no longer battle alone. There comes a point when we must reach out to another man or woman of God and seek agreement, and that covenant connection forms a threefold cord that is not easily broken (Eccles. 4:12), a connection that guarantees answered prayer. It is not often that we, as women, feel confident to ask for what we need. But this is a season when we cannot afford not to get the help and support we need, especially from those in positions of authority. We need to form alliances among ourselves and with men of God who know how to support, mentor, and encourage us as we fulfill our God-given assignments.

There is power in agreement. Jesus said, "If two believers on earth agree [that is, are of one mind, in harmony] about anything that they ask [within the will of God], it will be done for them by My Father in heaven" (Matt. 18:19, AMP).

We are stronger together. One can chase a thousand; two can put ten thousand to flight (Deut. 32:30). The enemies of jealousy, envy, covetousness, compromise, and criticism try to get us into a place of shame, rejection, depression, anxiety, insecurity, bitterness, and despair. These enemies press in closer and closer, increasing the pressure as the battle goes on. While Hannahs have supernatural strength to endure, there is no substitute for the power of agreement among believers on earth. God has established some unlikely destiny partners for Hannahs to help us bring forth the seed of promise and then help us bring it into the public eye for service as unto the Lord.

Prayers That Defeat Jealousy and Bitterness

Father, I make a decision to forgive. I forgive those who persecute me. Forgiveness is nigh, even in my mouth. Forgiveness is not a feeling but a spiritual act. Even though I don't feel like it, I use my will and forgive. Holy Spirit, help me release those jealous people who have hated me without cause. I give up my right to be right. I will not rehearse the painful words spoken to me. I use the power to forgive to free myself from the bondage of shame and rejection. I release love to those who persecute me. I release joy and happiness to those who are jealous of me. Lord, make my critics happy! I decree, "Father, forgive them; for they know not what they do" (Luke 23:34, KJV).

Declarations and Decrees That Defeat Jealousy and Bitterness

I bind every demonic spirit released against me by jealous people.

I break the assignment of spirits that come to harass and taunt me, in Jesus' name. I loose myself from fear and anxiety.

I decree that every negative word spoken against me falls to the ground and dies.

I will not be depressed, but I walk in the joy of the Lord. I decree that the joy of the Lord is my strength (Neh. 8:10).

I will not be oppressed or depressed by demonic forces released by negative, ignorant people. I will not retaliate, for vengeance is the Lord's, and He will repay (Heb. 10:30).

"Anger rests in the bosom of fools" (Eccles. 7:9). *I am a wise woman, and I will not be angry.*

Purge my heart from defilement. I will not let evil communication corrupt my good manners.

Lord, You are the One who breaks my adversaries in pieces. Lord, deal with my adversaries as You see fit. I ask that out of heaven You will thunder upon them. You will judge the ends of the earth and give strength to and exalt the horn of Your anointed (1 Sam. 2:10).

Declarations and Decrees About Not Compromising

But you, [woman] of God: Run for your life from all this. Pursue a righteous life—a life of wonder, faith, love, steadiness, courtesy. Run hard and fast in the faith. Seize the eternal life, the life you were called to, the life you so fervently embraced in the presence of so many witnesses.

—1 TIMOTHY 6:12, MSG

I will not settle for less than God promised for my life.

I will fight the good fight of faith and lay hold of everything promised (1 Tim. 6:12).

I will not give up on my dream or visions.

I will pursue, overtake, and recover everything promised to me.

I will not be divided in my heart about what You have promised me.

I will seek You with all my heart and find everything You've promised.

I pledge my allegiance to Your Word, Jesus. You will find faith in my heart.

I loose myself from doubt and unbelief.

I loose myself from the fear of being disappointed.

I loose myself from the opinions of others.

I believe that God "is a rewarder of those who diligently seek Him" (Heb. 11:6).

Chapter 6

MORE THAN A CONQUEROR

Hannah prayed and said, "My heart rejoices and triumphs in the LORD; my horn (strength) is lifted up in the LORD, my mouth has opened wide [to speak boldly] against my enemies, because I rejoice in Your salvation. There is no one holy like the LORD, there is no one besides You, there is no Rock like our God.

—1 Samuel 2:1–2, AMP

KNOWING THAT GOD is our Deliverer and our Rock, that He is our salvation, that He is fighting for us, and that He is with us releases us to contend all the more for breakthrough in the places where we are barren. Acknowledging that our undefeated God is on our side sustains our hope and trust during the fruitless seasons. That God wins every battle He enters should fill us with strength and confidence that we too are more than conquerors with Him on our side.

If you've ever had to endure a hard task, a long-term project at work or in your business, or a challenging season of any kind, then you know the value of having a special friend, coworker, teammate, or loved one who stays with you through the ups and downs, praying with you, working beside you, making you laugh, keeping you encouraged, and reminding you of the positive end results. Somehow the presence of one who holds the same or a higher level of strength charges your faith and gives you the stamina you need to complete the task and come through tough seasons on top.

The Bible says that God is the ultimate partner in times like this. He is a very present help (Ps. 46:1). We know that when God is with us, we have nothing to fear (Ps. 23:4). When God is for us, what can man do to us (Ps. 118:6)? Greater is He who is in us than he who is in the world (1 John 4:4). The Lord of heaven's armies defeats all His enemies; therefore, we win when He is on our side.

We must get a picture of this: God our Defender, God our Deliverer, the One who fights our battles and wins. He is the undefeatable warrior who is on *your* side! This is a revelation that we can have as Hannahs in this season. We have the unique opportunity to access what Hannah learned right where we are. We can know God as our Deliverer and Defender while the battle is raging to give us the strength we need to hold on until we see the fulfillment of God's promises.

Stand Still and See the Salvation of the Lord

I hear the Lord saying to you, dear Hannah, that no matter what you are looking at right now, these are the days of unusual, tremendous, unprecedented breakthrough. The Lord is calling you to go to a higher level of expectancy. He wants you to have an unshakable faith that He will deliver to you the seed for which you have been crying. It will be birthed. It will come to life. Through your tears God wants you to set your eyes on His faithfulness to deliver and break you out of seasons of barrenness, nonproductiveness, unfruitfulness, infertility, and lack. No matter what it looks like on the surface, no matter the taunts of your enemies, and no matter the attempts loved ones make to get you to settle and compromise, God is telling you to stand fast.

You are more than a conqueror. All you need to do is position yourself to see the salvation of the Lord.

Second Chronicles 20:1–2 says:

> The people of Moab with the people of Ammon, and others with them besides the Ammonites, came to battle against Jehoshaphat. Then some came and told Jehoshaphat, saying, "A great multitude is coming against you from beyond the sea, from Syria; and they are in Hazazon Tamar" (which is En Gedi).
> —2 CHRONICLES 20:1–2

The devil is always trying to gather people against your destiny. We've seen it in Hannah's story: Peninnah; Hannah's husband, Elkanah; and even the priest Eli had some way of challenging Hannah's faith in God's promise. You know whom the Lord has highlighted in your life as people who may not have the right understanding about your purpose. Some just don't get it. Others think you're crazy. And still others are just plain jealous.

Understand that God is a master strategist. He always has a strategy. And I believe that God loves to show off. God likes to demonstrate His glory. He doesn't like to hide anything. I believe God is getting ready to show you off and show Himself strong in your life.

Maybe you have felt as if everybody can see your failure. Everybody can see that you are still waiting on God after all these years of seemingly unanswered prayer. Like Hannah, your season of barrenness is obvious. Your life is not showing any fruit in a particular area. Daily you battle self-pity, shame, and unworthiness. But these are the days God is breaking that spirit of self-pity and shame and returning increase and multiplication to your life. He is causing you to see the enemies of your soul and bringing you to a place where you will know how to set yourself to seek the Lord first. We must look to Jesus, the author and finisher of our faith. Second Chronicles 20:2 talks about a great multitude forming against God's people. I don't care what it looks like, and I don't care how big the army is—Jesus is always the answer. God has a plan for your victory.

Let's look at 2 Chronicles 20, which gives us a ten-step battle plan for defeating the enemies that gather against the Hannah anointing. God highlighted this chapter in the Bible to me some time ago, and I believe it gives us one of the best models for victory and how to maintain faith and trust in God while enduring until deliverance comes.

1. Fear the Lord; proclaim a fast.

> And Jehoshaphat feared, and set himself to seek the
> Lord, and proclaimed a fast throughout all Judah.
> —2 Chronicles 20:3

This fear that Jehoshaphat felt was not the fear we normally assume one would feel when enemies begin to form. Jehoshaphat was responding to the spirit of the fear of the Lord. He knew that only God could stop that big army from coming against him, so he set himself to seek the Lord by proclaiming a fast.

Though it is not emphatically stated in Hannah's story, I like to think of the time when she couldn't eat and pushed back from the table as a time of fasting for her. The Bible says, "She wept and did not eat" (1 Sam. 1:7).

This is a season when Hannahs must fast and pray and seek the Lord. I don't care how big the problem is. When we take everything before God—no matter what's happening in our lives— fasting will help us see that nothing is bigger than God. Fasting enlarges our image of God and increases our ability to hear from Him and be submitted and obedient to Him.

The Bible doesn't say how long Hannah went without food, but there are records of three-, seven-, ten-, twenty-one-, and forty-day fasts that God's leading men and women undertook. How long you fast is not as important as your commitment to God that you will submit your flesh to His lordship. The duration of your fast is not as important as coming to the revelation deep in your soul that God is bigger.

Fasting may be a new thing for you, just as the difficulties in this barren season are unlike anything you've ever faced. You may not need to commit to a forty-day fast. Pray. Ask God. Be led by His Spirit. It was the Spirit of God that led Jesus into the wilderness, where He fasted and prayed for forty days. God also sent angels to minister to Him when He was at His weakest (Mark 1:12–13).

This may just be your hour to fast. Maybe you just need to fast for one day, just twenty-four hours to set some time aside so you can get in the right place to receive from God. Humility is the place or position you want to be in to see the grace of God overtake you. The Bible says that God gives grace to the humble (Jas. 4:6). Fasting humbles your soul. It puts your flesh in the battle so that whatever you have in your life that is not like God will bow. We talked about those little foxes earlier, in chapter 4. So push away from the table, shut off the television, log out of social media, and get in a quiet, humble place before God so you can hear His instructions for this battle you are in.

2. Remind yourself of who God is, and remind God of His promises.

> Then Jehoshaphat stood in the assembly of Judah and Jerusalem, in the house of the LORD, before the new court, and said: "O LORD God of our fathers, are You not God in heaven, and do You not rule over all the kingdoms

of the nations, and in Your hand is there not power and
might, so that no one is able to withstand You? Are You
not our God, who drove out the inhabitants of this land
before Your people Israel, and gave it to the descendants
of Abraham Your friend forever?"

—2 Chronicles 20:5–7

You have to remind yourself of who God is. Our world is
full of distractions, but we must focus on God and study and
know Him. Your default in times and seasons when the enemy is
coming against you like a flood needs to be that God—the God
of heaven and earth, who was and is and is to come—is fighting
for you and will win.

Once you have reminded yourself of who God is, remind God
of His promises to you. Jehoshaphat reminded God of His promises. He made declarations before the people and said who God
is. This is not just naming it and claiming it, and blabbing and
grabbing. These are the days to proclaim the name of the Lord,
even in your winter season, and to remember who God is. When
you do that, you magnify Him above your situation.

God is about to put a new glory on praise because praise is
the voice of faith. When you praise God, you are declaring that
you know Him, trust Him, and believe Him. When you can't
praise God, it's because you don't know who He is and your faith
is wavering. If you are having trouble lifting up praise to God
in the midst of your barrenness, I believe that God is going to
heal your faith. He's going to take your faith to another level. I
prophesy that the gift of faith is being released in this hour and
God is going to cause the high praises to be in your mouth and
two-edged sword to be in your hand, to execute the vengeance
that's written (Ps. 149:6–7).

3. Let the warrior within you arise to hear God's strategy.

> And they dwell in it, and have built You a sanctuary in
> it for Your name, saying, "If disaster comes upon us—
> sword, judgment, pestilence, or famine—we will stand
> before this temple and in Your presence (for Your name
> is in this temple), and cry out to You in our affliction,
> and You will hear and save."
> —2 CHRONICLES 20:8–9

As you come to understand the Lord's strategies for you in this season, I challenge you to wake up and speak to the warrior inside of you. Let that warrior understand that whatever the enemy is saying against you won't work. The Bible says that we should not be ignorant of the enemy's schemes (2 Cor. 2:11). You should have a level of discernment and know when the devil is taking aim at you. If you've walked with God for some time, then you may be getting to a place where you understand how the spirit realm works. You already know that when you're ready to break through into something, the devil starts talking to you: "It's not going to work. You won't break through. God is not going to come through for you this time. Don't waste your time praying and fasting and praising and worshipping. It's too late for you. Your time has passed. Nobody wants to hear your voice."

I like to step back when I hear the devil talking to me. I might let him talk for a day because I need to hear what he's saying and discern what's coming against me. But once I get a revelation of what weapon he's sending, I cry out to the Lord because He will hear and save. I listen for the strategy of the Lord and look in the arsenal of weapons He provided me, and I go to war.

You must do the same thing. The Lord will give you a revelation on how He wants you to stand against your enemies. Do not be afraid. He has trained your hands for war. The psalmist says it like this:

> He trains my hands for war, so that my arms can bend a bow of bronze. You have also given me the shield of Your salvation, and Your right hand upholds and sustains me; Your gentleness [Your gracious response when I pray] makes me great. You enlarge the path beneath me and make my steps secure, so that my feet will not slip. I pursued my enemies and overtook them; and I did not turn back until they were consumed. I shattered them so that they were not able to rise; they fell [wounded] under my feet. For You have encircled me with strength for the battle; You have subdued under me those who rose up against me.
>
> —Psalm 18:34–39, amp

Let the spirit of this passage arise within you in this season. Call forth that warrior, look at your enemy boldly in the eye, and say, "Are you trying to seduce me, devil? Are you mad because it's my time? Are you trying to convince me and say there's nothing for me? Well, there must be something for me, because if there wasn't, you wouldn't be saying anything." Let him know that you have an unshakable faith and you know it is going to work because God is faithful to complete the work that He has begun in you (Phil. 1:6).

4. Cry out for justice and wait for God's judgment.

> O our God, will You not judge them? For we have no power against this great multitude that is coming against us; nor do we know what to do, but our eyes are upon You.
>
> —2 Chronicles 20:12

God is going to judge the enemies of your soul, those who have come against you. To be clear, I'm talking about demons and devils, not people. Remember, "we do not wrestle against flesh and blood, but against principalities, against powers, against the rulers of the darkness" in high places (Eph. 6:12). At the end of the day it's not about people, and it's not even about you. It's about the call of God that's inside of you. It's about the assignment on your life. The devil is trying to stop it by releasing an evil unseen multitude against you—spirits of jealousy, rejection, compromise, judgment or criticism, shame, and pride and retaliation.

But these are the days when you will see God's justice. God is getting ready to judge your enemies. He says, "Justice is getting ready to roll like a river in your life." (See Amos 5:24.) But the problem is, many of us don't cry out for justice. Justice is "the maintenance or administration of what is just [or right] especially by the impartial adjustment of conflicting claims or the assignment of merited rewards or punishments."[1] Note the part that says "impartial adjustment of conflicting claims." This means God is going to look at the claims brought against you. He is going to hear your petitions for deliverance and protection from your enemies, and He is going to judge what is rightfully yours. And as you are in Him, everything He has belongs to you. So if the enemy took your fruit, if he came after your drive and motivation, if he came after your dreams, your blessings, your opportunities, and your provision, God is going to see that you get back what is owed to you. Not only that, He is also going to assign reward or punishment to the disputing parties according to what they deserve. Since you are covered by the blood of Jesus, all He sees is that you are in the right; all He sees is His favor, grace, and righteousness upon your life. He looks at your enemies, and He has already determined their end.

You must use your spiritual weapons in this hour. When you

come before the Lord seeking His justice, you are calling for Him to make a judgment against your enemies once and for all. Once He does, He releases the breaker anointing to set you free from their bondage and torment. With this revelation you can declare the day of breakthrough and justice.

5. Release a spirit of praise, worship, and glory in advance of the victory.

> Now all Judah, with their little ones, their wives, and their children, stood before the LORD. Then the Spirit of the LORD came upon Jahaziel…a Levite of the sons of Asaph, in the midst of the assembly.
> —2 CHRONICLES 20:13–14

Look what happened: God was trying to restore a principle back into His house and among His people. He wanted to release the spirit of praise and worship and glory. When the people stood before the Lord, the Spirit of the Lord came. We see here that a Levite of Asaph proclaimed the word of the Lord. These are the days when we must get back to praise and worship. The two-way exchange between God and us will always include praise and worship. It is not just for our weekly church gatherings. God is looking for Hannahs who will worship Him all by themselves, even if others misunderstand. He is looking for Hannahs who will get up from the table, go stand before the Lord, and meditate on who He is. We must position ourselves to worship God because worship opens the communication portal between us and heaven so that we can hear the voice of the Lord.

6. Do not be afraid or discouraged.

> Thus says the LORD to you: "Do not be afraid nor dismayed because of this great multitude."
>
> —2 CHRONICLES 20:15

We know that being afraid is about fear. But dismayed is when you lose courage and you lose all hope. But God says, "Do not be afraid." I have been meditating on this. The devil is like a roaring lion. He is always roaring; he's always saying something. But God says do not be afraid or dismayed. In Joshua 1:9 He says, "Have I not commanded you? Be strong and of good courage; do not be afraid, nor be dismayed, for the LORD your God is with you wherever you go." The devil can roar all he wants, but we have no reason to fear because the Lord is always with us; He will never leave us or forsake us (Deut. 31:6). He will silence the enemy (Ps. 8:2). He loves us with a perfect love, and perfect love casts out fear (1 John 4:18).

7. Take your position and stand still.

> Thus says the LORD to you: "Do not be afraid nor dismayed because of this great multitude, for the battle is not yours, but God's. Tomorrow go down against them. They will surely come up.... You will not need to fight in this battle. Position yourselves, stand still and see the salvation of the LORD, who is with you, O Judah and Jerusalem!" Do not fear or be dismayed; tomorrow go out against them, for the LORD is with you.
>
> —2 CHRONICLES 20:15–17

We love the song about the battle not being ours but God's, but I want us to take a fresh look. I don't want you to just hear it in the spirit from which you are used to hearing or singing it.

Let your eyes, ears, and heart be opened right now. As a prophet of God, I'm telling you there are some things you are not going to have to fight. You'll take your position as if you are getting ready to attack, but God is saying, "Just stand still." This doesn't quite seem like warrior behavior. I know because I am a warrior too. I know how to pick up what needs to be picked up. I know how to bind, loose, and sling anointing oil. I know how to put petroleum jelly on my face as the boxers do, put my hair in a bun, take off my earrings, and square up. But what about those times when the Lord says, "Calm down. I don't want you to do that this time"? When we seek the Lord, we know when it is time to stand and see God fight the battle for us.

8. Believe God.

> As they went out, Jehoshaphat stood and said, "Hear me, O Judah, and you inhabitants of Jerusalem! Believe and trust in the Lord your God and you will be established (secure). Believe and trust in His prophets and succeed."
> —2 Chronicles 20:20, amp

Sometimes our hearing becomes dull after hearing the same promises over and over. Sometimes we lose that freshness of insight and revelation we first had when we read or heard the Word of God. We read it, we hear it, we say it aloud with the pastor in church, but it's not penetrating our spirit. But just as Jehoshaphat said to the people of Israel, we too need to believe God. Yes, you've heard it before, but don't take that command lightly. In seasons of barrenness, when it seems as if we pray and pray without tangible manifestation, the devil works hard to attack our faith because he knows it is the key to our victory.

By faith we are going into a good land—a land of promise

and fulfillment—no matter what we have been up against, no matter what things looked like in the past or how insurmountable the situation looks. I come to tell you as a prophet of the Lord: believe God that you will walk in victory and the fullness of His promises.

I pray for a fresh spirit of revelation to come upon your life concerning hearing the word of the Lord. I rebuke all dullness of hearing. Let she who has an ear hear what the Lord is saying: "Believe Me, and believe what I am saying about your destiny."

You will hear clearly. Command those voices of doubt, insecurity, defeat, failure, taunting, and torment to be silenced in the name of Jesus. May the Spirit of God come and clear the spiritual airways so that you will hear the word of the Lord for your life. The voices that proclaim cancer, diabetes, infertility, anxiety, stress, and depression will be silenced. Believe God for wholeness and health. He is the healer. He will judge these enemies and set you free. The Bible says that every tongue that rises against you will be condemned (Isa. 54:17). Believe in the Lord your God, and you will be established and secure. Believe His prophets, and you will succeed.

9. Worship again.

Now hear this: the voice of faith sounds like praise.

> And when he had consulted with the people, he appointed those who should sing to the LORD, and who should praise the beauty of holiness, as they went out before the army and were saying: "Praise the LORD, for His mercy endures forever." Now when they began to sing and to praise, the LORD set ambushes against the people of Ammon, Moab, and Mount Seir, who had come against Judah; and they were defeated.
>
> —2 CHRONICLES 20:21–22

Because the people heard the word of the Lord and believed the God who spoke them, they were able to look their enemies in their faces and still release a voice of praise. The battle had not even begun. The enemies were still gathering. But Jehoshaphat appointed the worshippers to go ahead of the army to sing praises of thanksgiving to the Lord for what had not yet happened in the natural. They were able to praise God in advance because they believed Him. When they began to sing and to praise the Lord, He set ambushes against the people of Ammon.

Praise is the voice of faith. When we truly believe God, we have the undefeated One in our corner. When we believe God, we have the victory before the battle starts. Praise is the corresponding reaction to faith. So if you're not praising, you don't have faith. Praise the Lord, for His mercy endures forever! Some of us get so distracted by the Peninnahs, Elkanahs, and Elis in our lives that we can't hear God to believe what He is saying about us and our situation. Then when we come into the sanctuary, into the place of praise and worship, we barely open our mouths or lift our hands. Don't let Peninnah steal your praise.

Listen, this isn't hard. This is about a simple, childlike faith. Childlike faith takes God at His word and believes that He is and that He is a rewarder. Childlike faith causes us to praise God in advance. Childlike faith releases God to set an ambush against all its enemies.

Let me share what the Lord showed me. As I prayed for a fresh revelation of what God wants us to know about this verse in 2 Chronicles, I kept seeing all these angels. Every time I saw an angel, the Lord said, "Your praise dispenses angels." Then He showed me that this is how ambushes are set against your enemies—the angels assigned to minister to the children of God set the ambushes. Angels are warriors in the spirit realm.

Angels respond when Hannahs praise and pray. I am going

to discuss this more in the next chapter, but I want to introduce it here so you can understand the heavenly resources at your disposal. When you open up your mouth and praise the Lord, angels start moving on your behalf. When you praise and magnify the Lord, God releases a new company of angels. He says, "These are the angels of My presence. These are the angels of your destiny. These are the angels for your assignment."

The Lord showed me that there are certain angels that move with you. Then there are those that will be appointed to assist you in your specific assignment. This is why it is so important to know who you are, what you have been called to do, and how God has purposed the fruit you will produce. You may still be trying to hear what God is saying concerning the seed He wants to impart to you. You may still be battling the other voices sent to distract you, so you are having trouble hearing the voice of the Lord. And you can't praise just yet. God is saying to you, "I'm awakening your ears to hear. I'm going to give you new assignments. I'm going to open up new doors. As you tune in to hear My voice and silence all others, you will release praise for what you know I will do for you. I'm going to set ambushes against your enemies."

I see it so clearly for God's Hannahs in this hour. As it was with Paul and Silas, when you praise and pray, angels are going to kick open prison doors. Hinges are going to be blown off the doors of opportunity when you praise. When you say, "The Lord is good, and His mercy endures forever," angels will be dispatched, ambushes will be set, and the enemy will be defeated. There will be no trace left. You will not have to keep looking over your shoulder.

> So when Judah came to a place overlooking the wilderness, they looked toward the multitude; and there

were their dead bodies, fallen on the earth. No one had escaped.

—2 Chronicles 20:24

10. Collect the spoils.

When Jehoshaphat and his people came to take their spoil, they found much among them, including equipment, garments, and valuable things which they took for themselves, more than they could carry away; so much that they spent three days gathering the spoil.

—2 Chronicles 20:25, amp

To the victor go the spoils. God is highlighting this passage in this season to tell us to get ready for a great transfer of wealth. His Word says, "The wealth of the sinner is laid up for the just" (Prov. 13:22, kjv), but I am believing that it will no longer be laid up. I believe that God is getting ready to transfer the wealth, the abundance, the fruit to you. But you will have to go get it.

Though you may not be able to see the full picture now, modern-day Hannahs are going to come into a season of such wealth and abundance that they will not be able to hold it all themselves. We have families, houses, office buildings, and cities. We have people to send to school. We have charities to fund and develop. God will bless us with more than we can hold so we can sow our seed into the earth to make a big kingdom impact. This is the nature of our forerunner, Hannah.

Hannah cried out to God year after year for one son, but the Bible says that she had six children in all (1 Sam. 2:21). With Hannah's victory came more children than she could hold. We have to think big and break that "small" mentality. What God blesses us with from the hands of the wicked will take a while for us to gather. God is going to release to us a three-day blessing. It's going to take us three days in the spirit to gather it all in.

These are days of a great transference of wealth. God is going to defeat our enemies and lay them at our feet with all that has been laid up for us. All we have to do is gather it up.

Your Valley of Berachah

> On the fourth day they assembled in the Valley of Berachah, for there they blessed the Lord.... They returned...to Jerusalem with joy, for the Lord had made them rejoice over their enemies.... Then the realm of Jehoshaphat was quiet, for his God gave him rest all around.
>
> —2 Chronicles 20:26–27, 30

Berachah is a physical location with a spiritual meaning. The word means blessing, prosperity, praise of God, or treaty of peace.[2] Berachah is a place of prosperity and longevity. It means to be endued with power and prosperity and longevity for success.[3] God is taking you to your valley of Berachah, where you will be endued with power for longevity, success, and prosperity. Berachah also means to be endued with power to produce an abundance of offspring. Earlier we talked about how God has chosen you to bear fruit that remains. Do you see the connection here? Your blessing, breakthrough, and victory will not come one minute and be gone the next. What God is releasing to you will last. It will remain.

This and so much more can be released when we understand that praise is one of our most powerful weapons. In this season you are in, the enemy has tried to take the praise out of your mouth. He wants to silence you. All these years, you have been serving the Lord, presenting your request to Him, crying out, and holding out hope. I'm here to declare to you that today is a day of breakthrough. You will overcome your enemies. With

God on your side, the fight is fixed. You win, and the winner takes all.

I believe that for modern-day Hannahs this next season of blessing and fulfillment is also a time of vindication and justice. God says, "My justice is getting ready to roll like a river in your life." No matter what you're going through, God wants you to stand still and see the salvation of the Lord. Victory is near, and the spoils are yours.

Prayer for the Valley of Berachah

Lord, I thank You for taking me to the valley of Berachah—the place of blessing, fruitfulness, and breakthrough. I declare this is my season of vindication and recompense. The Lord will bless me with success and longevity. The Lord will show Himself strong on my behalf. I will stand still and see the salvation of the Lord! Lord, reveal Yourself as my defender. I thank You for fighting for me. You are my refuge and strength. You are a very present help in a time of trouble. I give You glory and praise. I lift up my voice with shouts of praise and victory. Father, I ask that You reveal Your power on a scale never seen before. Arise, O Lord, and demonstrate Your power. Arise, O Lord, and let the enemy be scattered. From the rising of the sun to the going down of the same, Your name is to be praised.

Chapter 7

HELP FROM THE SANCTUARY—
STRENGTH FROM ZION

May the LORD answer you (David) in the day of trouble! May
the name of the God of Jacob set you securely on high [and
defend you in battle]! May He send you help from the sanctuary (His dwelling place) and support and strengthen you
from Zion! May He remember all your meal offerings and
accept your burnt offering. Selah. May He grant you your
heart's desire and fulfill all your plans.

—Psalm 20:1–4, AMP

THE SANCTUARY, OR the temple of the Lord, has a special place
in Hannah's story. It was her refuge from the taunts of her rival
Peninnah. It was where she prayed, worshipped, surrendered to
God's timing, found her destiny partner in the priest Eli, and
received full restoration of the grace and favor that was the essence
of her identity. The sanctuary was a place of strength, encourage-
ment, and realignment. It was the place of her breakthrough.

I believe that in this season modern-day Hannahs will experience the significance of the sanctuary and of Zion (the city of
God, where the sanctuary is) in a whole new way. Not only will
we find shelter from the enemy, communion with God, and a
place to praise and worship, but it will be the place from which
God will dispatch our supernatural help in the form of angels,

send an increased anointing, and stretch out His hand to deliver us out of the hands of our enemies.

Before I get into the help that comes from the sanctuary of God, I want to point out one thing for the Hannahs fighting through shame and condemnation and believing the lie of the enemy that they are not worthy enough for God to reach down from heaven to defend and bless them: in Psalm 20:1 the psalmist calls on "the God of Jacob," not "the God of Israel," as one might expect.

If you recall, Jacob wrestled with the angel of the Lord, and his name was changed to Israel (Gen. 32:28). So why didn't the psalmist call on the God of Israel? Jacob stole his brother's birthright. Jacob made mistakes and came from a dysfunctional family. But guess what? Jacob was still defended by God. Angels were dispatched from heaven to assist Jacob and bring him revelation of the plan of God for his life. If you read the full account in Genesis 32, you will see how the psalmist is able to say, "May the name of the God of Jacob...defend you."

We Hannahs may tend to want to look at who we were in a past season and try to find justification for why we may not be hearing from God in our barren season. Shame and condemnation may cause us to think that because we aren't perfect, God will not bless us and make us fruitful. But if God answered and defended Jacob, He will answer and defend you against all your enemies, no matter what mistakes you may have made or how dysfunctional your family or what you may have done in your past.

Angelic Assistance

Psalm 20:1–2 says, "May the Lord answer you in the day of trouble; may the name of the God of Jacob defend you; may He send you help from the sanctuary, and strengthen you out of Zion." I love this psalm—it is one of my favorites. I could write a whole book on the revelation God has given me on it. But for now I want to bring some insight into how it relates to your breakthrough into fruitfulness and overcoming the enemies that gather during your season of barrenness.

As God has been talking to me about this psalm, I hear Him saying that this is a season of angels when He will release angels of destiny and breakthrough—angels that are encamped around us to deliver us (Ps. 34:7). These angels are specifically assigned to help you move into a season of great manifestation—unusual, unprecedented, and uncommon breakthrough and manifestation in your life. In Psalm 20 God talks about sending us help from His sanctuary. I believe this help is angelic help.

Every time God is ready to move in our lives, the anointing that accompanies our dreams, calls, and destinies increases, and angelic activity also increases. Some have said that when you go to new levels, there are new devils. The truth is, the more you are awakened to your destiny and what God is trying to birth in you, the more the enemy tries to stop it. But I want you to know that God will send helpers from His sanctuary. He will give His angels charge over you (Ps. 91:11). The Amplified Bible says it like this: "For He will command His angels in regard to you, to protect and defend and guard you in all your ways."

You are not in this alone. You are on an assignment from God. You are doing what you have been designed to do. God knows the enemies that rise up against you as you follow Him. So not only is He with you, but He also has angels assigned to you. Angels are "sent forth to minister for them who shall be heirs of salvation" (Heb. 1:14, KJV). The word *minister* means to attend, aid, or serve.[1] Angels are helpers, guardians, and protectors (Ps. 91:11–12); proclaimers, as with the birth of Christ (Luke 2:8–14); dispersers of revelation, as with the prophets Daniel, Isaiah, Ezekiel, and even the apostle John; executors of the divine will and justice of God (Rev. 12–16); and instruments of healing (John 5:4) and miracles (Acts 5:19; 12:7). Angels perform these necessary works on our behalf to aid us during seasons that are necessary for our development as we align with God to walk in our destinies. They help us break through barriers and traps the enemy sets up to stop us. In this season pray that God will dispatch His ministers of flames and fire to help you, that they will come and bear you up and bring strength to you from Zion.

An Increase of Strength and Anointing

Another way God sends help is by increasing the anointing in your life. Whatever you have been called to do, God has released an anointing on you to do it. Isn't that good news? The anointing breaks the yoke of bondage on our lives.

> And it shall come to pass in that day, that his burden shall be taken away from off thy shoulder, and his yoke from off thy neck, and the yoke shall be destroyed because of the anointing.
> —Isaiah 10:27, kjv

As God teaches you and prepares your heart for multiplication and increase, He is increasing that Hannah anointing within you, the anointing to be relentless in prayer, resistant against the attack of the enemy, and resilient in the face of opposition.

The anointing of God comes with supernatural empowerment from the Spirit of God—strength from Zion. The original language in the Old and New Testaments handles the word *anointing* slightly differently, but there is significance to each meaning. In the New Testament the Greek word for *anointing* refers to special endowments or gifts from the Spirit of God. It also means unction[2]—a word we don't use in our everyday speech outside of the church, but it refers to spiritual fervor or intensity with which something is carried out.[3] The anointing is a special strength or force given by God.

The Hebrew word for *anointing*, which can also be translated as "fatness," has the connotation that the yoke of burden or bondage is broken, from the fact a fat ox could break and cast off its yoke.[4] So in Isaiah 10:27 it is this sense of fatness, enlargement, or richness that breaks the yoke. This concept of anointing also refers to a fruitful or fertile land. As you grow, increase, and multiply in your anointing or strength from God, you become too large and too great for the yoke of the enemy to fit around your life. You break out of the bondage as the Lord increases and strengthens you. How powerful is that!

You may be feeling tired and worn down, but God is sending His anointed strength from Zion to lift you up, to make you too large and powerful for the enemy to bind up. He says that His strength is made perfect in our weakness (2 Cor. 12:9). So in this season let His strength and His anointing be made perfect in you. Let Him make you abundant in the anointing that He has called you to. Know that even in this season of seeming lack and barrenness, you are increasing and getting stronger day by day.

Rewards From the Sanctuary

The Lord also sends help from the sanctuary by remembering our offerings and sacrifices and rewarding us. In Psalm 20:3 (this is my favorite part) it says, "May he remember all your offerings and regard with favor your burnt sacrifices!" (ESV). Did you know God keeps good records? Whatever you've given, whatever you've sacrificed in the kingdom, God will remember and will reward you. He did this for Hannah, and He will do it for His Hannahs today. Hannah returned to His presence year after year. She brought offerings and sacrifices before Him. She brought her heart, tears, and petitions before the Lord because she knew who God was. She prayed: "O Lord of hosts, if You will indeed look on the affliction of Your maidservant and remember me, and not forget Your maidservant" (1 Sam. 1:11).

Psalm 20:3 reflects and confirms a promise to us, the seed of Abraham. I love this. As those with the Hannah anointing do, you have been getting up early in the morning, seeking the Lord, returning to His presence day after day, year after year. You have offered sacrifices of praise and generosity even in your season of fruitlessness. You've touched and agreed with others. You've sown seeds of kindness, finances, and other charitable works that people may not know about. I decree to you that this is the day God will start remembering.

Though He never forgets us, the Word says, "Put Me in remembrance; let us plead together; state your cause, that you may be justified" (Isa. 43:26, mev). God wants us to come to Him, reminding Him of our sacrifices and of His promises concerning us. He wants to reason with us. Though He doesn't forget, God values our recognition of His power and our empowerment through Him. Just as Moses, Abraham, and Jacob contended with God, you can remind God of what you've sown and how you've served; you can remind Him of His promises, letting Him know specifically what promises you are claiming. Add to your prayers even now that God would remember the offerings and sacrifices you made for the kingdom and its purposes: God, remember and forget not Your maidservants.

Learn how to receive your heart's desire.

There are times when we may feel as if we just need to work hard at fulfilling God's purpose for our lives and not ask for things we would like God to fulfill for us. But do you know that God will fulfill your heart's desires? Psalm 20:4 says, "May he grant you your heart's desire and fulfill all your plans!" (esv). That is powerful. There are things in your heart that you want just because you're you. God is going to fulfill it. Why? Because He put the desire in you. Remember what the Lord says: "Delight yourself in the LORD, and he will give you the desires of your heart" (Psalm 37:4, ESV).

You've been praying. You've been in the presence of God. You've been sowing and serving. These are the actions of a woman who delights herself in God even as she waits for the full measure of His blessing. You've been asking God to bless you with a seed that you can turn right around and dedicate to Him. You've been asking the Lord what He has designed you to do. What is the meaning of the season of barrenness? What does He have for you in this time? You are seeking Him and His will for your life. You are one who delights herself in the Lord.

Do you desire a home of your own, a loved one to be saved, or to plant a church? As long as your desire is holy, God will grant it. You don't need to settle or reduce the size of your desire. I break the spirit of settling. I join my faith with yours today that God will give you what you desire.

Purify your motives.

Heaven or hell can be in your desires; it's true. Hannah went through a process of seeking and praying and aligning, and then her desire came in line with the holiness of God. She had been coming into the presence of God—His temple—year after year before she offered the very thing she desired most back to God. That is when we know that our desires are His desires. So I decree right now, as I believe that God wants to give us the desires of our hearts, that all ungodly desires would die. Pray this with me, Hannah:

> *Let every ungodly desire and every lust of the flesh be broken in the name of Jesus. Let them die. Create in me*

a clean heart, and renew a right spirit in me, O God.
Because I am healed and delivered, I only have godly
desires. Lord, I'm praying that in this season of reward
You would reward my faithfulness, in Jesus' name. Amen.

When your heart is clean and pure, you can purely ask God for the things that you desire. I pray that you will open your heart and receive. Women know how to give and give, but do we know how to receive? I'm decreeing that you will learn in this season how to receive the love and favor of God without apology.

The Saving Strength of God's Right Hand

God stretches His hand down to you from His sanctuary to strengthen and deliver you. The psalmist says, "Now I know that the LORD saves His anointed; He will answer him from His holy heaven with the saving strength of His right hand" (Psalm 20:6). The hand of the Lord represents a supernatural endowment to do what you have been designed to do. God releases from His hand the spirit of might. Might is the impetus, or force, to do great exploits for the Lord. Miracles, signs, and wonders will flow into your life.

Destroyed enemies

When the hand of God comes upon you, there is new authority and power to destroy the enemies of your destiny. Exodus 15:6 says, "Your right hand, O LORD, is glorious in power; Your right hand, O LORD, shatters the enemy" (AMP). I decree that the hand of the Lord will touch your life. Let His power come upon you to do great exploits for the kingdom. I decree that every enemy of your soul is destroyed by the right hand of God!

Broken limitations

With the Creator of the heavens and earth as your partner, all things become possible. What is impossible with man is possible with God. Think about that, beloved Hannah. Limitations, barrenness, fruitlessness, and nonproductiveness are broken! A mantle will come upon your life, and you will do supernatural things. You will bear new things in the spirit and in the natural. Though they said you would not be able to give birth, the saving strength of the hand of God will reach down to you from His holy sanctuary, and new life will spring forth.

Think about what happened in 1 Kings 18:46—the hand of the Lord came upon Elijah, and he outran the chariots of Ahab! Prophetically, chariots represent something of great power and speed, something man-made, both concrete and abstract, such as the systems of this world. When the hand of the Lord is upon your life, you will overcome every man-made system or structure designed to stop your destiny.

Psalm 20:7 reads: "Some trust in chariots, and some in horses; but we will remember the name of the LORD our God." Again, chariots, and even horses, represent fast-moving, man-made systems or solutions. But we will not put trust in our own strength or abilities. We will trust in the Lord. Sometimes it feels easier to fall to our own systems of belief and doing things. We struggle with God's will and way at times. But this is why we have these seasons of winter, of barrenness. The Lord is teaching us and renewing our minds and spirits so that they will line up with His plans and purposes for our lives. As the Scripture says, "Trust in the LORD with all your heart, and lean not on your own understanding; in all your ways acknowledge Him, and He will direct your paths" (Prov. 3:5–6, MEV).

Acceleration and advancement

God's hand will bring acceleration. When God sends help from the sanctuary and His hand rests upon you, both acceleration and advancement come into your life. Stagnation breaks off. Barrenness breaks off. With God it is not by might or by power, but it's by His Spirit that we will accomplish all that He has set out for us to do (Zech. 4:6). His Spirit brings power that propels us forward. His Spirit brings us favor that allows us to advance beyond what we are naturally worthy of. May the strength of God come upon you. May the hand of the Lord rest upon you to advance you forward. Have you ever seen people who are in a season when it seems as if they just catapult from one place to the next? Though there may be a lot of things that go on behind the scenes that we do not see, that is evidence that the hand of the Lord is on them. And if He did for them, He will do it for you.

Stamina and endurance

When the hand of the Lord comes upon your life, there is an anointing of stamina and endurance released into your life. Isaiah 41:10 demonstrates this truth: "I will strengthen you, be assured I will help you; I will certainly take hold of you with My righteous right hand [a hand of justice, of power, of victory, of salvation]" (AMP).

Endurance is one of the key traits of the Hannah anointing. You may be feeling left behind, overwhelmed, discouraged, or rejected. You may feel that you are wasting your prayers and God isn't listening, but I challenge you to press in to that anointing and pray even more. Pray that the hand of the Lord will come upon you and supernaturally strengthen your life. Let endurance rest upon your soul. The hand of the Lord has come to impart to you the ability to finish your course with joy! As Hannah declared, those who stumble are girded with strength by the right hand of the Lord (1 Sam. 2:4).

Redemption and restoration

God will use supernatural empowerment to redeem and restore your life. In the Bible the right hand of God is used to describe the ways that the Lord will save, deliver, and rescue His people from all their enemies. It represents power and strength, redemption and restoration.

> Though I walk in the midst of trouble, You will revive me; You will stretch out Your hand against the wrath of my enemies, and Your right hand will save me.
>
> —PSALM 138:7

> The LORD said to my Lord, "Sit at My right hand, till I make Your enemies Your footstool."
>
> —PSALM 110:1

Hannahs Move the Hand of God

When you pray from your position as a modern-day Hannah, you are praying from a place of favor. The anointing to pray and never give up is the essence of the Hannah anointing. God honors the prayers of Hannahs with His faithfulness to answer. He breaks through our barren seasons to bring us help and deliverance from His holy sanctuary.

By your relentless actions, enduring prayers, and prophetic decrees, you move the hand of God. It's not hard for God to save His righteous ones and look upon them with favor because even in your winter season you delight in the Lord. You seek Him while He may be found. You desire to know God and His perfect will regarding your petitions. You desire to know yourself and God's destiny for your life. You desire to see yourself through His eyes. You are breaking free from self-condemnation, self-pity, and shame. You want to use the things you are praying for to change the world. You look forward to being blessed so that you can be more of a blessing. This is what you've been mandated to do.

So your prayers are partner-level prayers. You desire to partner with God to expand His kingdom and to make His name great. God moves quickly to respond to those whose hearts are after His. So even when you do not understand the hand of God, trust Him. Even when you think He's not going to come when you think He should, trust God's heart toward you. Know He loves you, that He will never leave you or forsake you. Understand how much He wants you to succeed.

God has a growth schedule for your life, and He wants to send you the help you need. His whole plan to deliver and save you was birthed out of love and His desire to be with you. He wants to commune with you. He sent His only begotten Son to die in a successful effort to make a way for us to be near Him again. I pray that you would understand the depth, the width, the height, and the breadth of God's love for you. I pray that you will know how your tearful prayers touch His heart and move His hand. He will answer you and send you help from the sanctuary.

Your Mouth Is a Great Weapon

Hannah used her mouth to pray and release prophetic decrees that invoked God's power, which gave her victory over the enemy's attacks. She said, "My heart rejoiceth in the LORD, mine horn is exalted in the LORD: my mouth is enlarged over mine enemies; because I rejoice in thy salvation" (1 Sam. 2:1, KJV).

That our mouths are a great weapon is not something we often hear as women, unless it is connected to our mouths being a destructive force. Sometimes we are told that our mouths will get us in trouble, that one word from us will tear things down, or that if we speak, we are rebellious or out of order. Silence is often the preference for women, both inside the church and out. We are often warned about speaking too freely, being too loud, and articulating our thoughts, input, and opinions. In meetings our observations, strategies, and ideas are at times ignored. In church our preaching and teaching are carefully limited to sharing with other women and children. It is to the disadvantage of organizations and groups that a woman's voice is silenced more times than it is encouraged to be released.

Women, like anyone, have spoken foolishly. We see evidence of this from Paul's letter to the church at Corinth. (See 1 Corinthians 14.) But women's voices are of critical importance in this season. Yes, we need to use discernment about when to speak and when to be silent, but our prayers, prophetic declarations, and praise speak forth the strength and deliverance of God. When we call out to God, He hears us and answers. The earth is desperate for what we are praying for. What we are decreeing brings life and light. What we prophesy with our mouths releases the word of the Lord over generations of people.

Job 22:28 says, "Thou shalt also decree a thing, and it shall be established unto thee" (KJV). The word translated "thing" means "speech, word, saying, promise, command."[5] The word translated "established" means to arise, confirm, make good, perform, or succeed. It also means to raise, set up, erect, or build.[6] When you use your mouth to decree the Word of God, you are building, constructing, and activating the promises with your words. The mouth is important in bringing forth the promises of God. God enlarged Hannah's mouth over her enemies. Her mouth released her breakthrough.

The only weapon in the armor of God is the sword of the Spirit, which is the Word of God (Eph. 6:17). Words from the Word are the most powerful ones we can speak. I think speaking truth, life, and blessing from the Word is of critical importance in a season of barrenness. Whenever there is barrenness in your life, use your mouth as a weapon. Your voice silences the taunts and torments of the enemy. Hebrews 4:12 says the Word of God is quick, powerful, and sharper than any two-edged sword. The sword of the Spirit is the quickened Word of God for your situation. When you are praying to the Lord for an answer to a problem, an idea for a business, or a child the way Hannah did, the Lord will quicken a scripture in your spirit from His heart or mouth. This *rhema* word is considered a single-edged blade proceeding out of the mouth of God. When you declare this word by faith, it becomes a two-edged sword that releases the power of God in your life. I admonish you to fill your heart with the Word of God and pray in the Spirit, allowing the Holy Spirit to quicken words in your heart that will cut and destroy the works of the enemy in your life.

As humans we are created in the image of God, and the tool He used to create and conquer was His voice. God tells us through Scripture that He creates the fruit of the lips (Isa. 57:19). The cry of the barren is for a seed. The cry of the barren is, "Give me a son or daughter, or else I will die." Hannahs are not content with the status quo; they are desperate to continue the bloodline. They are desperate to see multiplication of the kingdom agenda.

You must be persistent in your prayers and petitions to God. Use your authority to declare what He has said about you and your dreams. Use your voice to sing and give Him praise and thanksgiving for doing the impossible in your life. Praise is a weapon that breaks the backs of your enemies that arise. Use your voice to bind what is not of God and loose the benefits of the heavenly sanctuary in the earthly realm.

When you're waiting on the promise of God to be fulfilled, enemies such as shame, rejection, compromise, and even jealousy will attack your mind. Many times when you're not succeeding the way you thought you would or your dreams are not coming to pass the way you thought they would, the enemy comes at you with a conspiracy of silence. He makes you turn the volume down on your confession of faith. He tries to make you feel as if you didn't hear God correctly and that you are not needed where you are. He will try to make you think you're not called to a certain ministry or that you shouldn't leave your job to start a business. These voices of doubt aim to move you out of your God-ordained position so your voice will be silenced. The enemy does not want your influence to be the catalyst for change that it will be if you open your mouth.

I decree to you, Hannah, open your mouth, call for help from heaven, see angels dispatched to rescue and assist, watch the hand of God move in the earth on your behalf, listen for your enemies to be silenced, and get ready for fulfillment, increase, and multiplication.

Prayers That Dispatch Angels

When praying for angelic assistance, it's important to remember that angels hearken to the voice of God's word (Ps. 103:20). We cannot command heavenly angels to do anything that is not in agreement with God's Word, purpose, plan, or will. As heirs of salvation, it is important to connect our voices to God's Word—to pray and declare the heart and mind of the Lord for our lives primarily using Scripture. Our prayers can include words of Scripture, words of prophecy, and the promises of God. The Holy Spirit is responsible for governing the activity of angels as we pray and decree the word. The Holy Spirit gives us the unction to pray the right words for every season of our lives.

> Lord, I thank You for giving Your angels charge over
> me. They bear me up in their hands, lest I dash my

foot against a stone. I decree that angels are ascending and descending in my life. They are hearkening to, listening to, and obeying the voice of God's word in my life. Lord, let Your angels go before me, making every crooked place straight and every rough place smooth. I loose angels to open doors of opportunity for me. Let the angels that arrange divine connections and supernatural encounters be loosed in my life in Jesus' name. Let angels contend with every adversary at every God-ordained open door. In the name of Jesus I loose the angels of my anointing. Lord, I ask that You send angels to stir the river of healing in my life. I decree life in my womb. I decree fruitfulness. Father, I ask that angelic activity would be increased exponentially in my life. I decree that angels of prosperity and ministers of finance are released to help finance kingdom assignments in my life. Lord, release the ministering spirits that are sent to minister to the heir of salvation. I decree angelic announcement and divine instruction will be delivered from heaven to me. Even as the angels came and gave Daniel skill to understand, Lord, I ask that You will send angels of revelation to my life. Father, I ask that You will send ministering flames of fire to take coal from the altar of heaven and purge my iniquity.

Prayers That Call Down Help From the Heavenly Sanctuary

Lord, I set my heart to understand Your will for my life. I humble myself before You. Let the words of my mouth and meditations of my heart be acceptable in Your sight. Let my words be heard on high, and send help from the sanctuary. Lord, I humble myself and cry out to You.

I need Your help and Your strength. Your strength is made perfect in my weakness. Incline Your ear to my prayer, O Lord. I ask for supernatural strength to endure to see the promise fulfilled in my life. Strengthen me out of Zion to finish the work set before me. I ask for fresh anointing and the new wine of the Spirit to fill me up. Holy Spirit, strengthen me with might in my inner man. I declare I am strong in the Lord and the power of His might! I delight myself in You, so I ask that You fulfill the heavenly desires in my heart. I declare that I will love You, O Lord, my strength. You are my steadfast, secure place, my fortress that I run into and am safe, my Rock, and my Deliverer.

Prayers That Release the Hand of God

God, I place every part of my life in Your dependable hands. I declare no one will snatch me out of Your hand. Your hand is strong and mighty. Lord, things You have asked of me are outside of my own abilities. I am totally dependent on Your hand to touch my womb and bring forth a child. I am totally dependent on Your supernatural empowerment to produce extraordinary things in my life. I lean in to You. I surrender my will to Your will. Work in me to will and do Your good pleasure. Lord, I cry out for Your hand to be with me and keep me free from pain. Let Your hand empower me with a supernatural grace that redeems and restores my life from destruction. Lord, stretch out Your hand and fight against my enemies. I decree that Your right hand and holy arm have given me the victory. Open Your hand and satisfy my desire. Where Your hand leads me, I will follow.

Chapter 8

PROVOKED INTO DESTINY

> Hannah's rival provoked her bitterly...because the Lord had left her childless.
>
> —1 Samuel 1:6, AMP

You NOW HAVE an understanding of all the pieces of the Hannah anointing you hold within you, which are necessary to break through. You are at the brink of something phenomenal. Do not lose heart. I am praying that God will enlighten the eyes of your understanding. You have Hannah as a model for what to do when you are all alone in a house full of people who make fun of, make light of, or misunderstand your dreams. She is the model for how to stand strong when no one understands. Hannah didn't have someone to pattern her strategic exit from her season of barrenness after. But we do have Hannah, and we are in a company of thousands of other Hannahs who will stand together until we see our deliverance come and our vindication rise like the noonday sun (Ps. 37:6). As you stand fast in this place of faith, hope, and expectancy, grab hold of what God is saying, and exercise and execute the things He is telling you to do.

Hannah prayed for a son, but her conception and delivery time were delayed while God developed in her the wisdom and fortitude to be able to raise the greatest prophet the world had ever known. God wanted her to be whole and wholly aligned with His divine purpose for the desire He placed in her.

It has been noted that "one of the greatest prophets that ever lived came out of Hannah's womb because somebody provoked her....Peninnah means...jewel, precious, valuable....The most valuable thing in Hannah's life was the thing that provoked her to cry out to God for more."[1] Another pastor noted, "Like Hannah, you have been provoked to purpose by your friends, your loved ones, every word goes inside of you like a sword. Don't give up. God is using those provocations to thrust you to your purpose."[2]

I am not the woman of God I am today because my life has been easy. I have been betrayed, falsely accused, and gossiped about. I've learned that every flower grows through some dirt. I made a choice to allow my pain to transform me into a vessel fit for the Master's use. I decree a great unveiling of your purpose. There are anointings, dreams, and visions waiting to be birthed in your life. Let them come forth and change the world! Now is your season of breakthrough!

Birth is a painful and sometimes ugly process. There are people yelling at you to push, and sometimes friends and family seem like the enemy during the process. But your destiny partners are provoking you into your destiny. Peninnah had little idea that she was reinforcing Hannah's faith by continually declaring that Hannah's condition was purposed by the Lord, but this foundational element allows us to hold on to hope when despair is creeping in the door. Knowing that every detail of our lives is ordered by the Lord gives us reassurance that He is with us.

What hardships, relationships, or attacks from the enemy are pushing you into your destiny? Let your answer form gratitude in your heart to God for ordering everything toward seeing you fulfill your purpose. Let God inhabit your praise.

Let the Cry of the Barren Arise

Give me children, or else I die!

—GENESIS 30:1

For too long in our culture the blessing and beauty of motherhood and the essence of what it means to be a woman have been under attack. Sexual abuse and misconduct against women have affected how we see the beauty of fertility and the blessing of being a woman. Unwanted pregnancies have come against the beauty of birth and nurturing, but I decree that the cry of the barren is rising. Women are once again crying out to bear sons and daughters who will change the world as we know it.

Because of rejection and the fight to balance gender inequalities, our views of the value of motherhood and of children have been skewed. What was once a strength and a blessing has become a weakness and a curse. There is a hardness of heart toward the beauty of motherhood, of raising and nurturing children. Women have been hurt and limited because of this unique ability for centuries. We've been sidelined, passed over, pushed to the background, and shut out of opportunities, and our words and perspective have been silenced because of this beautiful, God-given gift. The ability to create and sustain new life should never be diminished.

I declare to you that the desire to reproduce and bear sons and daughters is returning to the hearts of women in this season. Anointed with grace and humility, we are pushing back against the toxicity of gender inequality and are no longer giving place to the enemy concerning our ability to bear fruit that remains. The fruit of our womb has been appointed "over the nations and over the kingdoms, to uproot and break down, to destroy and to overthrow, to build and to plant" (Jer. 1:10, AMP). This is the purpose of every natural, spiritual, financial, charitable, corporate, or literary Samuel a Hannah will birth in this season and the seasons to come. The enemy will no longer have free rein to snuff out and abort the dreams and gifts God has given especially to us. God will heal our hearts in this area and return to us the time and fruit that the locusts have eaten.

The desperation to birth the promise of God is intense because of what that seed will be set in the earth to do. Both natural and spiritual children have significance in carrying forth the inheritance of the saints. The maternal instinct is returning to the land.

Fulfill Your Vow, and Position Your Seed for Success

Once our promised seed has been birthed or fulfilled, there is rejoicing, yes, but also there is responsibility. Once our God-sized dreams and purpose have been birthed, we cannot forget the vow we made to God: "O LORD of hosts, if You will indeed look on the affliction (suffering) of Your maidservant and remember, and not forget Your maidservant, but will give Your maidservant a son, then I will give him to the LORD all the days of his life" (1 Sam. 1:11, AMP). How will we give back to God a seed that is worthy of its call? How will we nurture it and position it for success?

After Hannah gave birth to Samuel, she did not rush back to the temple. She did not rush to hand him off to a nursemaid or nanny. She stayed with him and nursed him until he was fully weaned:

> Then the man Elkanah and all his household went up to offer to the LORD the yearly sacrifice and pay his vow. But Hannah did not go up, for she said to her husband, "I will not go up until the child is weaned; and then I will bring him, so that he may appear before the LORD and remain there as long as he lives."
>
> Elkanah her husband said to her, "Do what seems best to you. Wait until you have weaned him; only may the LORD establish and confirm His word."
>
> So the woman remained [behind] and nursed her son until she weaned him. Now when she had weaned

him, she took him up with her, along with a three-year-
old bull, an ephah of flour, and a leather bottle of wine
[to pour over the burnt offering for a sweet fragrance],
and she brought Samuel to the LORD's house in Shiloh,
although the child was young.

—1 SAMUEL 1:21–24, AMP

Hannah fulfilled her vow by dedicating Samuel to the Lord.
Even though Samuel was her only child, "she was willing to give
and to trust God with all that she had. Her time in God's waiting
room had made her a woman of prayer and great faith."[3]

Hannah took time to position Samuel for success. Sometimes
we get what we've asked for from God, and as soon as it is delivered, we begin praying for a different thing. Think about taking
the full allotted time for maternity leave, both in the spirit and in
the natural. Because of fear of losing opportunity or provision of
some kind, women don't always take the time needed to nurture
and properly raise what God has given. I know this is not always
possible for new moms in the natural, but do not let fear dictate
how you will raise your child after he or she is born. Allow God
to bring about the mental and spiritual shift you need to wisely
pour into the seed you have so long desired.

Though many of us have to get right back to work physically,
Hannahs have that special anointing to focus in on the main
thing in the face of incomprehensible distraction. We are able to
set everything else aside and quietly tune out the noise in order
to nurture and steward the seed we labored for.

The Power of Silent Surrender

Sit in the place of honor at my right hand until I humble
your enemies, making them a footstool under your feet.

—PSALM 110:1, NLT

When a man's ways please the Lord, He makes even
his enemies to be at peace with him.
                                        —Proverbs 16:7

There are a great multitude of false voices speaking into our
lives. They are voices of torment, mocking, and accusation. These
voices are sent by the enemy to get you to doubt the word of the
Lord over your life. I'm here to tell you: Pull yourself away. Get up
from the table. Leave your food there. Do not engage in any fleshly
battles. No matter what the devil or your Peninnah is trying to
accuse you of, you must learn how to lay low. The devil wants to
put you in a fleshly battle where you're trying to prove and explain
yourself, sometimes even after you've received the victory.

I can only imagine what it may have been like for Hannah the
moment she gave birth. Maybe she was momentarily tempted to
show Samuel off to Peninnah. But that is not what we see. She
still held her peace and did not try to redeem herself. We cannot
go from a place in the Spirit, where we are aligned with the purposes of God, to a place in our flesh, where we use our answered
prayers as a trinket of personal validation. That's pride. That's
selfishness. That is giving place to the enemy and letting our flesh
rule in our season of fulfillment. Women of God, we cannot do
that. We have come too far and prayed too long to let a moment
of pride lead us to gloat in the faces of our enemies. Humility
and grace must still be our guide.

The Bible says there is a time and season for everything,
including a time to speak and a time to be silent (Eccles. 3:1, 7).
Once you've made your decree and prayed your prayer, there is a
time to stand still and see the salvation of the Lord. The Lord is
releasing a strong spirit of discernment on modern-day Hannahs.
They will not be unbalanced in their communications. The Holy
Spirit will set a watch over our mouths and keep the doors of our
lips that we will not sin with our words. The ears of modern-day

Hannahs will be open to the voice of God, and they will have the tongue of the learned, speaking right words in right seasons.

Silence was one of Hannah's strategies against her enemies. On some things we have to learn how to shut our mouths. Just pull back, surrender, and stay low on your face before God. Even after the fulfillment of God's promise, we must remain humble, knowing that it is God who gives seed to the sower. Everything we prayed for belongs to Him.

There isn't much credit a barren woman can take for suddenly bearing a child. It is all God. All we did, without really knowing how it would happen, is surrender it all to Him. The devil keeps trying to get us to walk in the flesh, but we must remain in a place of "I surrender all"—for real. Anytime you get tied up in arguments, self-preservation, vindication, and doubt, you are operating from an evil place: "Beware, brethren, lest there be in any of you an evil heart of unbelief in departing from the living God" (Heb. 3:12). We want to get all that evil, doubt, and unbelief out of us. There's no place for it on the path we are assigned to. We can trust God to defend us.

We are in a season when we really must understand the power of surrendering to God—our health, finances, children, everything. We cannot be in our flesh at all because God is getting ready to dispense justice. He is getting ready to pass His judgments against us and every tongue that has risen against us in condemnation. We can easily get on the wrong side of God's judgments if we allow our enemies to move us into our flesh.

You'll never know the blessing of surrendering to the judgments of God even when you've been treated unfairly—until you see your enemy in a position that could thrust you right into your destiny. You may never know the blessing of your humble and graceful silence when your enemy was launching vicious verbal attacks against you—until you see that he could connect you to kings and presidents. You may never know the blessing of your decision to bow down and worship God instead of telling that person where to go—until you see that person has been the key to your breakthrough all along.

You may be tempted to retaliate. You may even be wondering why your enemies are still prospering, but I encourage you to let the justice of the Lord roll like a river. Let God handle them. You keep your eyes on Jesus. If God were not a God of mercy and He carried out the full measure of His judgments against your enemies the way you want Him to, they would not be in place to connect you to that opportunity that will open up a tremendous, unprecedented door for you. I'm telling you, God will do what is just. He will do what is right.

God said, "Tell my Hannahs that I will open up My hand and satisfy their deepest desires and that the enemy they see in front of them will be the one through whom My purposes for their lives will be fulfilled."

These are days of great and unusual recompense. *Recompense* means you are going to get paid back from God and then some. It is a reward given for what was lost or harmed, a reward for your good efforts that were made. This is not about getting a blessing you haven't been looking for. Recompense is about stuff you're supposed to have.

God says to His Hannahs today, "Expect unusual recompense. I will vindicate and restore you. Everything that's been lost, everything that has been held back will be released to you. I am the Lord your God. I will repay."

> "Vengeance is Mine, I will repay," says the Lord.
> —ROMANS 12:19

Let God do it. You need only to be still.

This Is Your Season

It's time, Hannah. You are a carrier and deliverer of a promise that will release the power and glory of God in our lives and communities. It's time to trust God to open your womb. He has a set time for your promise to be birthed. It's time to harness the resistance, relentlessness, and resilience God has given you. It's time to know who God is and who you are. It's time to stand on God's promises and pray persistently until you bear fruit that remains. Your season of barrenness is ending. This is your season of fruitfulness because you have endured. Jealousy, rejection, compromise, judgment, and shame will not defeat you. You have been chosen by God. Stand still and see His salvation. Your promised seed is on the way. This is your season.

Prayer of Thankfulness and Exaltation

Lord, You are the One who kills and makes alive. I thank You for opening my womb. You have raised me up, and I worship You. You have set me among princes. Thank You that You've conquered and given me victory over my enemies. Great are You, Lord, and greatly to be praised. Lord, I give You everything that You've given me. You have fulfilled Your promises to me, and I bow before You in worship. Thank You for making all my dreams come true. Great is Your faithfulness! You are the Rock of my salvation. There is no one like You! Lord, You are my sun and shield. You have given me grace and glory. No good thing have You withheld from me. My soul makes its boast in You!

Notes

Introduction
You Are the Answer

1. New Spirit-Filled Life Bible, NKJV, ebook (Nashville, TN: Thomas Nelson, 2002), 1741.

2. Blue Letter Bible, s.v. "Channah," accessed December 3, 2018, https://www.blueletterbible.org/lang/lexicon/lexicon.cfm?Strongs=H2584&t=KJV.

3. Blue Letter Bible, s.v. "Channah."

4. Blue Letter Bible, s.v. "channowth," accessed December 3, 2018, https://www.blueletterbible.org/lang/lexicon/lexicon.cfm?Strongs=H2589&t=KJV.

5. Blue Letter Bible, s.v. "chanan," accessed December 3, 2018, https://www.blueletterbible.org/lang/lexicon/lexicon.cfm?Strongs=H2603.

Chapter 1
Closed for a Season

1. Michelle McClain-Walters, *The Deborah Anointing* (Lake Mary, FL: Charisma House, 2015), 13.

Chapter 2
Unanswered Prayer—Welcome the Wait

1. Bible Study Tools, s.v. "kairos," accessed December 3, 2018, https://www.biblestudytools.com/lexicons/greek/nas/kairos.html.

2. *Merriam-Webster*, s.v. "epoch," accessed December 3, 2018, https://www.merriam-webster.com/dictionary/epoch.

3. Bible Study Tools, s.v. "*hora*," accessed December 3, 2018, https://www.biblestudytools.com/lexicons/greek/nas/hora.html.

4. Blue Letter Bible, s.v. "*hōraios*," accessed December 3, 2018, https://www.blueletterbible.org/lang/lexicon/lexicon.cfm?Strongs=G5611&t=KJV.

5. "Waiting on the Lord," Bible.org, accessed December 6, 2018, https://bible.org/article/waiting-lord.

Chapter 3
Don't Grow Weary

1. *Merriam-Webster*, s.v. "relentless," accessed December 6, 2018, https://www.merriam-webster.com/dictionary/relentless; *Merriam-Webster*, s.v. "abatement," accessed December 6, 2018, https://www.merriam-webster.com/dictionary/abatement.

Chapter 4
The Remedy

1. *Merriam-Webster*, s.v. "breakthrough," accessed December 7, 2018, https://www.merriam-webster.com/dictionary/breakthrough.

2. Blue Letter Bible, s.v., "*menō*," accessed December 7, 2018, https://www.blueletterbible.org/lang/lexicon/lexicon.cfm?Strongs=G3306&t=KJV.

3. Michelle McClain-Walters, *The Anna Anointing* (Lake Mary, FL: Charisma House, 2017), 36–37. The definition of *meno* is quoted from Michelle Haarer, *Breaking the Barriers of the Impossible* (Bloomington, IN: WestBow, 2015), https://books.google.com/books/about/Breaking_the_Barriers_of_the_Impossible.html?id=OHalCwAAQBAJ.

Chapter 5
The Enemies That Gather

1. *Merriam-Webster*, s.v. "jealous," accessed December 7, 2018, https://www.merriam-webster.com/dictionary/jealous.

2. *Merriam-Webster*, s.v. "covetous," accessed December 7, 2018, https://www.merriam-webster.com/dictionary/covetous; *Merriam-Webster*, s.v. "envy," accessed December 7, 2018, https://www.merriam-webster.com/dictionary/envy.

3. Blue Letter Bible, s.v. "*tsarah*," accessed December 7, 2018, https://www.blueletterbible.org/lang/lexicon/lexicon.cfm?Strongs=H6869&t=KJV.

4. *Merriam-Webster*, s.v. "adversary," accessed December 7, 2018, https://www.merriam-webster.com/dictionary/adversary.

5. *Merriam-Webster*, s.v. "rival," accessed December 7, 2018, https://www.merriam-webster.com/dictionary/rival.

6. Blue Letter Bible, s.v. "*ka'ac*," accessed December 7, 2018, https://www.blueletterbible.org/lang/lexicon/lexicon.cfm?Strongs=H3707&t=KJV.

7. Eddie Foster, "How to Overcome Jealousy," *Insights Into Changing Your Life* (blog), January 24, 2013, https://lifehopeandtruth.com/change/blog/how-to-overcome-jealousy/.

8. *Collins Dictionary*, s.v. "compromise," accessed December 7, 2018, https://www.collinsdictionary.com/us/dictionary/english/compromise.

Chapter 6
More Than a Conqueror

1. *Merriam-Webster*, s.v. "justice," accessed December 7, 2018, https://www.merriam-webster.com/dictionary/justice.

2. Blue Letter Bible, s.v. "*Bĕrakah*," accessed December 7, 2018, https://www.blueletterbible.org/lang/lexicon/lexicon

.cfm?Strongs=H1294&t=KJV; Blue Letter Bible, s.v. "*Běrakah*," accessed December 7, 2018, https://www.blueletterbible.org/lang/lexicon/lexicon.cfm?strongs=H1293&t=KJV.

3. R. Laird Harris, Gleason L. Archer Jr., and Bruce K. Waltke, eds., *Theological Wordbook of the Old Testament* (Chicago: Moody Press, 2003), entry 285.

Chapter 7
Help From the Sanctuary—Strength From Zion

1. Blue Letter Bible, s.v. "*diakonia*," accessed December 10, 2018, https://www.blueletterbible.org/lang/lexicon/lexicon.cfm?Strongs=G1248&t=KJV.

2. Blue Letter Bible, s.v. "*chrisma*," accessed December 10, 2018, https://www.blueletterbible.org/lang/lexicon/lexicon.cfm?Strongs=G5545&t=KJV.

3. Merriam-Webster, s.v. "unction," accessed December 10, 2018, https://www.merriam-webster.com/dictionary/unction; Merriam-Webster, s.v. "fervor," accessed November 4, 2018, https://www.merriam-webster.com/dictionary/fervor.

4. Blue Letter Bible, s.v. "*shemen*," accessed December 10, 2018, https://www.blueletterbible.org/lang/lexicon/lexicon.cfm?page=1&strongs=H8081.

5. Blue Letter Bible, s.v. "'omer," accessed December 10, 2018, https://www.blueletterbible.org/lang/lexicon/lexicon.cfm?Strongs=H562&t=KJV.

6. Blue Letter Bible, s.v. "*quwm*," accessed December 10, 2018, https://www.blueletterbible.org/lang/lexicon/lexicon.cfm?Strongs=H6965&t=KJV.

Chapter 8
Provoked Into Destiny

1. Darrell G. Vaughn, "Maximum Impact," Battlefield Ministries, December 12, 2010, http://www.bmcog.org/sermons/dec/2010/impact_Aud.html?.

2. Shine Thomas, "Provoked Into Purpose," City Harvest AG Church, July 27, 2015, http://www.cityharvestagchurch.org/provoked-to-purpose.

3. Aduke Obey, "Provoked to Destiny," House of Refuge, May 15, 2011, http://www.houseofrefugeng.org/?cp=sermon.view&id=53.